For Mom, Dad, and Larry—
my guardian angels on this earth

Acknowledgements

I have been on a path of conscious soul work for the past thirty-one years, beginning with my writing of a high school paper at the age of seventeen on the book, *Siddhartha* (Bantam Classics, 1981), by Hermann Hesse. My acknowledgments begin in memory of this great and timeless author.

As I have moved further along in my conscious journey, I have been influenced by other gifted authors who are true visionaries and seers, lighting the path for all of us fortunate enough to have read their works. It would be impossible to name them all and how each has specifically contributed to my personal collective knowledge. Most prominently, I would like to thank James Redfield, Greg Braden, Marianne Williamson, Deepak Chopra, Don Miguel Ruiz, Kathy Hurley, Theodorre Donson (in memory), Jean Houston, Richard Moss, James Twyman, and Esther and Jerry Hicks channeling Abraham for sharing the gifts of their clarity and brilliance.

I would specifically like to thank Marianne Williamson for kindly granting me copyright permission to reprint her widely acclaimed poem, "Our Deepest Fear" from her book, *A Return to Love, Reflections on the Principles of "A Course in Miracles"* (Harper Collins, 1992). I would also like to thank Coleman Barks, a gifted scholar on the writings of Jalal ad-Din Muhammad Rumi for allowing me to print two writings of Rumi as per his interpretations.

I offer a special thank you to Tom Bird, a gifted author, whose writing retreat I attended to write the first draft of this book. Thank you, Tom, for helping me to write this book from the pure space of my heart.

I would also like to acknowledge the following personal teachers who have guided me in understanding and applying spiritual higher truths to my life: Jessica Dibb, Kathy Hurley, Theodorre Donson (in memory), Jasmine Hisha, Elizabeth Spear, Ron Sirchie, Rev. Barbara Mayerman, and the loving residents of the Shanti Mandir Ashram in Walden, New York. I would also like to acknowledge in loving memory, Peter Bloch, who taught me guiding principles of Siddha yoga and other aspects of Hinduism. He was truly an enlightened soul who walked this earth in unconditional love.

I offer a heartfelt thank you to my dear friend, Max Amichai Heppner, who lovingly offered his "eagle eye" to assist me in the editing of this book.

I have been a personal empowerment therapist for the past eighteen years, and would like to thank my clients for the emotional honesty and fortitude to have bravely faced their life's challenges and lessons. This commitment to their personal work has allowed me to go deeper in the messages I have been able to convey in this book, as we are students and teachers to each other.

Most importantly, I would like to thank my parents, Glenda and Joseph Appel, who instilled me with pure unconditional love from the first day of my life, and never once faltered in living and reflecting this ultimate truth of who we are. It is a divine gift to be their daughter, as there is not a greater and more powerful teacher than unconditional love. Equally, I would like to thank my brother, Larry Appel, who has been a guiding light, a best friend, and beacon at times when I have been lost.

Contents

List of Guided Meditations

(all guided meditations are available as audio downloads on the author's website at *www.ultimate-healing.com*)

A Note to the Reader

In this book, I invite you into your personal journey of living through love in the heart, and going deeper in your spiritual awakening. You are given insights for learning to keep yourself mentally, spiritually, and emotionally grounded, in order to live your life in a more fulfilling manner.

This is a journey book for fully arriving and living in a grounded place within your heart. It is a book that explains how living from that sacred space not only deeply heals you, but also the world around you. This is one of the most important, essential truths of living, and is the highest responsibility we have to ourselves and each other. It is the ultimate healing and the ultimate responsibility we have to ourselves and each other. I will explain, in depth, the essential messages and opportunities for this ultimate healing and the related journey in which we all participate.

This sacred journey begins with our divine God-connected selves at birth, as we are born into a state of knowing. We then move into a state of amnesia, where we become confused by the delusions of a false self, based in fear and ego protections. Coyote Trickster, the master ego shape-shifter, joins along the journey as the false self unfolds. The journey takes us into the soul lessons that we have contracted in this lifetime, where we navigate through the illusions of the fear-based self. A golden chariot arrives, driven by our higher self as our soul lessons unfold. Ultimately, this journey then returns us to the true heart-connected self and our original birth name, Clarity, who is guided by her sister, Grace.

During this journey, we create the reality by which we live via our free will. We do this by choosing the quality of emotional vibrations we send out into the world in every given moment. These vibrations begin with each one of us individually and become ever-expanding ripples of energy that then affect the world around us. In chapter three, I explain to you in detail about this "ripple effect," and weave its essential lessons and our responsibilities to them as the chapters unfold.

At various times, I provide guided meditations intended to

take you deeper into your soul journey, your healing, and your resolutions. For your convenience, I have made audio downloads of each of them available on my website, *www.ultimate-healing.com.*

I also share poetry I have written to encourage you to connect more deeply with the soul messages of this book—perhaps even your own inner poet. In a few instances, I share the poetry of other, well-known poets for the same reason.

I wrote the first draft of this book during a five-day writer's retreat called "The Tom Bird Method: Write Your Book in Five Days," in Sedona, Arizona, led by an accomplished and talented author named Tom Bird. I arrived at the retreat with a strong feeling of the themes I wanted to convey in writing, but I was open to a process that Tom referred to as writing from the "creative collective mind." This is instead of writing from the more typical left-brained critical and analytical side.

I could not have predicted that this book would become a "living" book for me. During my writing, some of the very soul lessons I convey for you here were popping up in the experience of the writer's retreat for me, as well as during revisions at home in Baltimore. This challenged me to go further and deeper into my own soul's journey toward resolution.

Knowing that there are no accidents and feeling attuned to the synchronous rhythms of our life experiences, I knew, beyond a doubt, that these meaningful lessons were meant to be shared with you and not just kept within. They were woven into the book as they occurred in the writing retreat and during revisions.

In my many years of work as a personal empowerment therapist, I have learned it is so often true that we teach what we have fully integrated into our own lives and sometimes what we are still in the process of integrating. The greatest teachings we can offer to each other come from the essence of these integrations. Our own stories bring us closest, in the soul lessons they carry, to the ensuing emotions we are challenged to work through.

For this reason, at various times, I will refer to additional personal experiences and their invitations for healing the emotions of the heart. This is intended to help connect you to those same universal themes of healing your heart. Through these personal stories, I will share what it is like to not get these essential truths of the heart, living your life instead in the confusion of the false self that is based in fear and ego protections. In sharing these lessons, I will also convey the pathway back to living through love in the heart.

These are stories I encourage all of you to relate to your own lives. They are an invitation to connect with your own personal stories and yourself more fully. As I unfold these stories, treat them as spiritual fables of the soul and hear the messages that are intended to bring you back to your own beautiful, God-given self.

I will often use the feminine voice when the third person is necessary and a choice between either gender is appropriate. In particular, when I refer to the name "Clarity"—who appears often in the book—please know her name is intended for both sexes.

If you are not living your life in a fulfilling way—if you are ever depressed, angry, uncertain, or sometimes scared, defensive, reactive, or blameful—then you are not living by example the essential truths of the heart. Again, this is the truth of our God-created, divine, beautiful selves and requires the dispelling of the illusion of the false self. I will share with you through some of my life stories how to fall out of love in order to return to the state of love that represents who we truly are.

I begin this book's journey with the voice of my younger self from late childhood, in her senior year of high school, speaking to me from her heart. You see, we all have a child self who lies within our adult beating hearts, and often carries the whispers of forgotten sacred expressions reflecting who we truly are. Within my child self, as you will soon see, were the whispers of a young writer waiting for so long to be valued and expressed.

Prelude – My Young Writer Speaks to Me

My young writer speaks to me:

Today is a celebration! It feels like my birthday even though my birth date is not today. Can we light a candle, a new kind of candle? It would be a candle to honor my wish that came true. You came back to me; you came home, and now we are together again! But there is a question that I pondered for so long...

Why did you leave me? I knew where we were going. I was already a master, didn't you know? I was so sensitive and in tune. At my young age, I had a way of speaking the truth, essential truths for living well. I loved to write and the words flowed. I was beautiful already.

Do you remember *Siddhartha*? In 1981, at the age of seventeen, I wrote your senior paper on its meaning. In it, I wrote, "Time and eternity, individualism and the universal self, and many other paradoxical onenesses create the harmony of man's existence." At the conclusion of the paper, I wrote, "Emphasis must be placed on the absolute importance of finding oneself. To live without a personal identity, life becomes purposeless, a game with no meaning. If a person cannot relate to himself, he will fail to relate to others. Self-discovery leads to a personal understanding of life and the human predicaments."

Why did you leave? Were you afraid of we, our power, who we really could be as one. Were you afraid we'd be alone, or maybe that we would be too much for the world? I felt this and I didn't want to overwhelm anyone. Did you feel it too?

One time I wrote, "Deep thinkers think beyond the punctuation point of logic." Do you remember? I was so excited and I ran down to the kitchen to read it to Mom. She just kind of stared at me. She did say, "Wow, that's really nice. You are so gifted, so extremely gifted." But I could tell she didn't get it. I felt sad and alone as I took the compliment from her that made me feel so far away. "Thank you, Mom," I said, as I choked down a heavy, pained feeling in my throat. I still wanted to write, and I continued on, but I felt the first seeds of fear, self-doubt, and an unfamiliar pang of isolation. Do you remember?

She and Dad loved me very much, though. We had this in common and were so lucky for this guiding light. Maybe that's how you were eventually able to return to me.

In 1986, in a moment of connection, you wrote "Into-me-see," a poem to me with love and remembrance, and I became hopeful of your permanent return:

I...
nestled in the tree, and then

into-me-see

a rushing flow of
dusty dormant childhood
transposed the moment and ...

we embraced

I hugged her rooted constancy,
cool and inviting,
a firm reassurance born of
divine connection

I nuzzled into her limbs
and felt her

nurturing warmth

soon...

I swung from her branch,
for an instant, suspended
and met her steady gaze.
I knew I would return again
for her to carry me.

You felt me then; you dipped your toes in, but you didn't stay very long. I waited and, several years later, I wrote a poem inviting you back to me. Do you remember it? I called it "Five Minutes to Enlightenment":

in here...in-a-box [boxed].
I've been waiting for so long for you now.
Come... now...don't be shy—
open the lid... yes... open now.
What do you see?
Come, silly... open your eyes.
Peer, gaze, allow...
you will not die from this, you see.
Into-me-see
come now...take my hand.
We could play for the rest of our lives...
where am I, you ask...?
Well, I'm right here as long as
you take my hand.
When you come to me, I am then real.
Come, come now, come.
Love me...
come.

It was mostly quiet for the past thirty years, though you tested the waters a bit and came for a visit now and then. When you went to that place in our soul where we would meet, it never took you long to reconnect with me. We flowed.

In 1998 you wrote your wish to reconnect with me, through "The Dunes." I thought you were beginning to find your way back and that you were getting closer to staying with me. You seemed tired of holding back on we.

I'm in the bottom of the cup
reaching up, sucking down,
for last, dear morsels of juice...

frozen, through the ice that formed
around my heart, like a hypothermic numb.

Quenching a parched desert
with a droplet of relief,
only the winds were known and felt.
Caressing, they were the nurturing loving gods
that said to the receiving sands,
"Let go, and we will make you."

...And the dunes obeyed,
swept high and rolled out low—
high and low, high and low—
sculpting a pristine vision of
surrender.

...The rhythmic meditation soothed.
Somewhere ice melted.
A heart thawed free.
A bird surfed the wind-gods,
celebrating the awakened dunes.

Light cast the re-birthed dunes.

Did you know they were golden?

I felt you wanting to reconnect with me, but
your journey through fear didn't seem to be over. I

watched you, and I saw this fear take hold of you.
I saw your life events unfolding and watched you
lose your sea legs. You seemed to react to yourself
with doubt, and then you mostly left. Yet, I was so
hopeful for your permanent return, and I patiently
continued to wait. Seven years later, in 2005, I
wrote to you "Eternally Yours":

> Until we meet again, my friend,
> I will leave these words for you.
> For I have been your guide all along
> in this journey everlasting.
> Sometimes you have found me in
> little scraps of wisdom prose
> scattered about your weary clothes.
> When you least expected it,
> I was lovingly there to remind you
> of you and who you really are, again
> and yet again. Never did I tire for you.
> I was in a workshop written line
> and in a heartfelt bridge of feelings
> phrased for others.
> I was even in your dreams,
> from the depths of your soul.
> I get in more easily when your
> sweet innocent ego is at rest in REM.
> Many times, you saw me for a split second,
> only to blink hazily again.
> This was okay, because I always accepted you
> and remained your most ultimate and loyal friend.
> Sometimes you saw me for a minute or two,

and on occasion, you even embraced me
and held me longer.
I was always there to shine for you
no matter how little or much you let me in.
Until we meet again, my friend,
know that I eternally walk beside you
until I walk fully within you.
It is me, my friend, for I am you.

We had the gift. I never stopped beating my heart through yours. I believed that if I beat strongly enough, my heart would be a beacon for yours, and you would return for me.

And now I'm so relieved and filled with joy. You have rejoined me and we can be one again. Flower power! Aren't those two wonderful words together? Now that we are together again, we can "flower." Flowers are never fearful. Take my hand now, in-to-me-see; you will not die from this you see.

...and I respond:

My dear child, it is true that you knew already what I chose to forget, only to rediscover it. You see, you knew before I was ready for these essential guiding truths of life. We were too young to understand them in a way that we could really apply. We needed the backdrop of life experience to learn why these truths were essential to begin with. You knew the essence, but I left for a while to go find out why. I went on a journey of amnesia only to reawaken. I didn't know it then, but it was so we could rejoin in a more complete way. Only life experience could give us that. We didn't know this; neither of us did, at least not consciously. But our heart knew and our higher guide pulled up in a golden chariot and took over the controls. It was a grand journey, and, as you know from waiting and listening, it was also at times a grand illusion.

I could not have done it without you, my child. It is true. You were beautiful already. You set the stage as the seer, and I became the navigator to enrich your truths with life experience. You wrote about "paradoxical onenesses" and that it "creates the harmony of man's existence." I went out into life to learn from the ultimate paradox; that of fear and love. In learning to resolve that paradox, I brought harmony back to you. Thank you for being so brave and going for the gusto, because now, my child, we truly have a message to share.

You wrote about the importance of "finding oneself" in order to have purpose and meaning in life. In my love for you, I went out to do that for us. It was the only way we could truly integrate your higher knowing and understand the "human predicaments" you were so wise to know existed.

I saved a compilation of poems you wrote once for a school project. You ended the compilation by writing, "I have not yet begun to write; life is here to guide my pen."

I gathered the ink for us. Let's begin...

Chapter One

The Journey and the Illusion Begin

You are a child of the universe. That is why you are here! I know of such a beautiful poem that describes this truth eloquently. Have you heard of it? It is called "Desiderata," by Max Erhmann. In one of the lines, he states, "You are a child of the universe, no less than the trees and the stars; you have a right to be here. And whether or not it is clear to you, no doubt the universe is unfolding as it should."

It is time to celebrate you! The rewards are great and you will feel great when you live in celebration of yourself. Guess what happens when you celebrate you? It makes other people want to do the same thing.

Funny, I spent so many years not really living from my own example, instead trying to tell people "like they are," how I thought they needed to be. Living by our own example is not only the most powerful conveyer of truth, but it is really the only thing that reaches the heart of another. I was missing this for so long in my life. Many of us are. I never meant to hurt anyone. Most of us didn't mean for this either. I was not grounded in love in the heart. Many of us are not. We all hurt other people, and most of all ourselves, when we do not express from our hearts, when we do not ground ourselves—and therefore our responses to the world—with love in the heart.

This life is a grand journey and a grand illusion. It is a journey of the greatest love story ever unfolded. The journey begins on the first day immediately following our birth, where we commence the long and painful process of losing our way from love—the divine love from which we arrived in a state of remembering who we truly are. We then enter into the grand illusion of the amnesic, fear-based, false self. This false self, also known as the small self, is a confused aspect of us that is separate from our divine nature. This happens to all of us in varying degrees. Each and every one of us writes our story and determines the ultimate course and conclusion. Throughout our lifetime, we choose whether we live lost in the fears and illusions of the false self or successfully return to the divine state of universal love and remembering, to complete this grand circle.

The grand journey is a journey home to the heart. On its road lie the potholes, detours, and signs toward reestablishing our heart connection, as well as experiencing and understanding what happens when we lose that connection. As we navigate this road, we learn how essential it is to cultivate and heal that connection as completely as we can. Along the way, we are presented with lessons on honoring and trusting our own personal inner guides, our higher-knowing selves, which we cannot do if we are not in a state of love. We are confronted with curves that challenge us to not give away our power and not to relate in anger. We are given many opportunities to find our ground and honor ourselves to stand in it. As we twist and turn on this road, we face or deface lessons of self-honesty, and take in or push away powerful lessons of what it really means to be fearlessly self-responsible.

We cannot resolve these challenges positively without self-love and the self-worthiness that accompanies it. The positive outcome of this grand journey requires the absolute cultivation of compassion toward ourselves and others—this softens our hearts into unconditional acceptance. It also requires absolute acknowledgement of others and the honoring of their truths without judgment—this softens their hearts into unconditional acceptance.

This journey teaches us what can happen when we move through life not grounded in the heart but instead lost in the grand illusion of fear. Fear is the small self trying to masquerade as the true, divine self. If it were a dog, it would be a Jack Russell terrier trying to pass as a Newfoundland. Fear is the grand illusion, the lost-ego shape-shifter that comes in the night to steal the divine truths of ourselves. It pretends to be the big *kahuna*, which in Hawaiian means "expert navigator."[1]

We can have all the truths in the world—even what we may call the highest truths—but we don't really have them if we are not grounded in the heart, in love. We can speak them in the head but we have not made the journey from our heads to our sacred beating hearts. Without this ultimate grounding, we will not feel the self-resolution and joy we deserve to feel in our beautiful and sacred lives. We will not be living fully alive. Instead, we will be living beside ourselves.

There are those who walk beside themselves and those who walk within themselves. Which one do you want to be? Which one are you willing to be? Do you have the courage to choose divine love over earth-based fear? Which one will give you the fulfilling life you want? Do you have the emotional and spiritual courage to walk fully within yourself?

Can you deal with the toxic shame that has built up in your life and blocked your way—to which you form your defenses, create your despair, cause your own separation, depression, and isolation? Are you ready to release the toxic shame that has blocked your golden, radiant doorway to love?

What happened to you along the path that scared you so, that knocked you off your balance? Isn't it worth letting go and resolving your deep-seated unworthiness to reunite with the beautiful loving being you truly are?   Who are you to deny yourself any longer? The world needs you! One of my soul teachers once explained to me that self-denial is actually a form of self-righteousness because, ironically, you have to make yourself pretty darn important in order to feel unworthy.

Try to disprove this simple but profound point. Self-love is the only thing that truly heals the spirit. Yes, self-love. Not the self-righteous type—that isn't self-love. That is self-abandonment. That comes from fear and smallness, and fear and smallness come from self-estrangement. True self-love is unconditional and it makes you laugh lovingly with acceptance of yourself. Authentic self-love allows you to forgive yourself and have compassion for yourself.

Self-forgiveness is not synonymous with irresponsibility; you need not hold yourself in contempt or in an emotional prison when you err. Self-forgiveness is an aspect of self-acceptance. It is the willingness to not live your life from a shame-based mindset, but actually a self-responsible mindset based out of self-worthiness. Cultivating self-love allows you to take in this precious life and not waste the beautiful moments we get. It allows you to be fully alive.

Think of yourself as living in the garden of your true, divine self and you are given a choice as the groundskeeper to plant and nurture the healthy seeds or get overwhelmed and lost by the weeds. We have accountability in this garden to clear out our own weeds and a responsibility to give love and life to our unique and individual seeds. These are the divine seeds of self, because we come into this life with them. They are God-given. When we nurture them, our true selves blossom and flourish. Needless to say, it would also appear quite silly if we distracted ourselves with others' weeds while standing in the responsibility of our own garden.

And, yes, of course self-love encompasses the love of others as well. But can you really get to a place of unconditional love for others before you have truly decided to love yourself? It is time for all of us to base our lives in inner and outer compassion, not compromised caring that is distracted by self-absorption. We must move away from the ego-based urges and insecure impulses of our small self to fix the people in our lives so that our world can be comfortable. Have you ever noticed how exhausting this is? Instead, we must first fix ourselves in love. Then we must compassionately and lovingly reach people in a heart-connected, and a no longer angry, way.

Anger is fear. You cannot express your truth in a way that people will want to listen to if you come from energies of anger, fear, and attempts to control others—all hidden under the veil of self-deception. Remember, the same truths can be verbally communicated but the entire energy vibration it conveys will be different. This anger/fear vibration will be subconsciously picked up by those receiving the message and is likely to create confusion. You cannot communicate to others in your life separated from your heart center and expect to reach the heart center of those who receive it.

Let's look even closer at the attachments of the small fear-based ego self and the inevitable, ensuing self-absorption and isolation this brings forth. The following metaphor illustrates this, as well as the unrealized egotism of anyone who becomes offended by such behavior in others while believing they are not caught up in these negative energy expenses. This metaphor uses a robot—a "unibot" in my example—to describe these states of mind, either in others or ourselves, because anyone in these states would be acting out of unconscious automatic impulses and *artificial* intelligence rather than *genuine* intelligence to deal with the unresolved hurts of life.

We live in a world with "unibots," and any one of us can also be a unibot. Unibots are those people who are in a complete state of self-absorption. Their universe is them and no one else can get in. They are in a perpetual state of fear-based small self, where their efforts to gain satisfaction are through attempts to make others behave and respond the way they want them to. They do not gain their sense of self through inner security but only through outer attempts to make others change for them. In this state, they become self-sabotaging "humanoids," addicted to negative thought patterns and projected false beliefs that their inner happiness is dependent upon the responses of others. They do all of this unconsciously. They are not actually trying to offend you, they are only trying to act like themselves. They have the lead role in their own drama and they are playing and perfecting their part.

So, do not be offended, because if you are, then you are in a state of egotism or self-importance. You would then be con-

fused, thinking it is about you when in fact it is only about them. And we know that you don't want to be a unibot, too!

On both sides of this equation, then, we must ask this honest question: Are you in a "uniship" or a relationship? Anyone in a uniship is lost in a relationship of one, and by definition, would be a self-absorbed unibot. True self-love and love of others would not do this, but the masquerading confused love of the scared small self would have us believe that the world needs to change for us, in this disempowered state. It is important that we all reality-check ourselves to recognize and remove any self-deceptive armor from our ego-confused selves and start living and truly relating.

A unibot, being self-absorbed, can only be in a uniship. And, after all, a ship of one is not much fun. Hey, where's the party....?! We must all be honest, careful and emotionally brave for ourselves. Realize that we cannot be in a conversation and say we are relating to the other person but keep bouncing the ball back to our own world. That is not a conversation; that is a "unisation," which is not very sensational. It will leave all parties exhausted as the tug-of-the-ego war transpires and both parties perspire.

We must all listen, engage, take true interest, and be in true relation. Then we will feel elation, not deflation!

This metaphor illustrates why we must cultivate compassion and acceptance in our relationships. We would then step out of our small self's absorption and into the field where we meet our fellow players as ourselves and begin to recognize that there is no separation. This reminds me of a beautiful affirming Mayan phrase of our oneness, *in lakech*, which means "I am another yourself; you are another myself." Let's get in touch with the oneness from which we are derived and share and hold that in its sacredness in our hearts. Then remember if you poop in your neighbor's pond, you have also pooped in your own. We are way too beautiful and sacred to do that to others and ourselves.

The words on these pages reflect the sacred truth of who you are so that you can no longer be scared. These are words to be honored and shared. It is time to see ourselves as one humanity with a collective heartbeat. In this way, we reconnect with the sacred wisdom from our souls and merge this with the life wisdom from our lessons of the heart and the misguided small self. We may then express through our God-reflected state of unconditional love. It is the completion of the grand circle that started in love, became lost in the small self and its fears, only to return to love again. It is the resolution of the grand journey and the grand illusion.

It is the ultimate healing and the highest responsibility we have to ourselves and each other to wake up and live with conscious intention toward this resolution. This is how we deeply heal ourselves as well as the world around us. Do you choose this lifetime?

Chapter Two

Love the 'Asshole' as Thyself

L et's go a little deeper and consider how our core beliefs were originally formed. These are beliefs that we carried from early childhood and into the autonomous adult world where we first begin expressing them. I will lead by example and encourage you to connect with your original stories as I share mine.

When I was a young adult, I truly meant well and I never meant to hurt anyone at all. I just thought that everyone wanted to own their mistakes; I was happy to point them out. But I was coming from a place of hurt and anger. I was mad at life and didn't know it, because I came from a loving family and the world did not seem to match up.

My original story formed and shaped my core beliefs of the world at large, as is true with all of our original stories. In my story, I was a child from a loving family where communication was valued; everyone was made to feel important and their individual feelings were made to count. We were a very emotionally expressive family that cried and laughed together. Above all, we accepted each other and forgave each other for our mistakes as we moved along in our lives. None of us were afraid to take ownership and responsibility for our errors, and we did not feel ashamed when we did this. We also complimented and acknowledged each other's accomplishments.

I went out into the world with a belief that everyone was like this. This is how we all create our beliefs regarding the outer world, from our original childhood family experiences. To connect with this in yourself, ask yourself, what was the strongest and most immediate belief you carried toward the world when you first stepped out into your independent life as a young adult? As a result of my original story, the world at large didn't seem as nice and loving as my family, and seemed to lack the ability to look in the mirror of self-accountability so readily.

I FELT DUPED! Was this some kind of cruel joke? I must come and save the world! They just don't realize the mistakes they are making, and I am here to correct them. Surely they won't mind; I'm sure they will be grateful and appreciate me. I know I can help them. I have come from such an unconditionally loving family...

Hey, what's going on here?! Why is everyone so mad at *me* when it's *them*? I didn't do anything wrong!! I'm only trying to help! I was annoyed, indignant, a victim lost in the scared small self. What a screwed-up world! I have to hurry up and change them all so we can live happily ever after. Wow!

It wasn't until much later in life that I realized my parents had probably felt mad at the world, too, at least as an undercurrent reserved for moments when others treated them badly. In other words, as a family, we could be loving as long as everyone behaved rightly, but if someone behaved wrongly, we were quick to judge or feel indignant. Not so unconditional, huh!

But, no offense to my family—most of us have come to a place within ourselves where we wanted the world around us to change, even if we got there in different ways. How did you get there? What was your story of childhood origin? What was your overriding core belief as you entered the world an independent adult?

If our original beliefs about the world were positive, we then became indignant and angry toward the shadow-side of the world where healing had not yet occurred. We may have then become impatient and intolerant of others with their blinders. Ironically, when our original beliefs about the world were negative and untrusting, we may have missed the beauty and love of the world that was right there before our very eyes. But we were too afraid to trust. How could this have been the same world? Hmm, it must then have been our internal world that made the difference in our perception.

Clearly the world at large was the same world in both cases. In the first example, it was easy to love when the world around us was loving, but it was not so easy to be loving when people were mean or seemingly insensitive or ignorant. In the second example, it was easy to miss the love that was there, thereby feeling unloved and becoming angry at the seemingly cruel world. Either way, we became angry and indignant when the world at large didn't match up with our expectations of it.

So, if it is so hard to love, then are we really mastering the truth of unconditional love? In a way, we might say, the ultimate challenge is in loving the "enemy." In order to do this we must forgive the "enemy," recognize the sameness within all of us, and realize that until we do that, we are our own ironic enemies. "Welcome to planet Earth; the joke's on us, unlimited!" But so is the beauty and divine grace of a magnificent way of life we may all share once we resolve this unintended illusion. Then the sign would read, "Welcome to planet Earth, land of the beloved."

I was trying very hard to master this at one point in my life and put customized license plate frames on my car to reflect this, so that every time I went out to my car I would be reminded of the lesson. The front license plate frame read, "Key to a good life…" The back license plate frame read my proclaimed answer, "…I love you, asshole." I lasted about a week with this message, slightly concerned about offending anyone, especially a police officer. "But, officer, I can explain..." Nah! Plus my sweet father and I had to switch cars that week, and I really couldn't imagine my father explaining that message to an officer! In all seriousness, though, remember we are our own enemies until we learn to let go of our expectations of others.

How do you do that? Part of the answer lies in compassion.

You can forgive someone of their ignorance and wish them healing, but be detached from personalizing their drama for at least two reasons: One, it is your definition of ignorance, jaded by your polarized view of the world, that you will invariably project into your relationships. How can you be sure that the person you encounter is behaving the way you think they are behaving? Is this the truth or your self-imposed projection? Is it then fabricated to protect you from the personal changes you may need to make?

This may help: always remember the difference between *intention* and *reception*. What others intend may not always be what you receive. So, ask yourself what truly is their intention before you draw any conclusion. The degree of your own ego-based attachments will determine your ability to move through these considerations honestly. If your truest answer is that their intention is loved-based, even if you don't like their behavior or method of communication, they are not really being mean or ignorant. They are just not responding the way you prefer. So who is being unloving, really? Do you see how this helps you connect your heart to theirs rather than your small self's ego to their small self's ego?

On the other hand, if you conclude that they weren't coming from a loving intention, and that they were intending to be hurtful, remember, as the metaphor in the first chapter illustrated, they are not trying to offend you. Rather, they are just trying to act like themselves and they have the lead role in their own self-projected drama to which they are playing their part! So why should you be offended? It is not about you, is it? If you are offended, you are taking personally what is really about them. Isn't it much better, then, to offer compassion?

This is likely to be silent compassion in your heart. Wish them healing, peace, and resolve; watch how it changes your response to them and then watch how it changes them. If they are not ready at all for change, I guarantee you this will at least quiet them and quiet their bad behavior. This is provided you are not throwing your own digs back into the ego mix and are remaining grounded in the heart, where compassion resides. Either way, you will feel so much better within your own spirit, rather than enduring the unpleasant feeling of taking them personally. This would only confuse them anyway and strengthen the defenses between you. I guarantee it. Let the war games continue or not.

By the way, you may be wondering about the back license plate's message and what I did after I removed it. I changed it to read, "Let your light shine." That looked really nice with my sweet father smiling behind the wheel.

Chapter Three

The Ripple Effect

Do you sense that there is a larger relationship here? The emotional energies of the world repeat from the smallest micro level to the largest macro level: from the inner self, to personal relationships, groups, communities, within countries, and then between countries. We live in a world of self-similarity. Patterns repeat themselves on all levels either in conflict or in harmony. All of the information in this book can be applied to resolving conflict or living harmoniously on any level. This is precisely why we must begin with ourselves. The first vibration always begins with the self.

What we send out into the world repeats on larger and larger levels. What ripple do you send out into the world that will then replicate more of the same vibrational energy in its expanding current? This is the essential truth of self-similarity and our ultimate responsibility! Doesn't that amplify hugely the importance of self-love and self-resolution?? Do you get it? What "ripple effect" are you responsible for, the one that creates war or the one that creates peace? Which one do you want to be a part of?

Let's consider a definition of the ripple effect: "A term used to describe a situation where, like the ever-expanding ripples across water, when an object is dropped into it, an effect from the initial state can be followed out incrementally."[2] So here, the "object" is our thoughts, their accompanying emotions, and the indestructible power of our collective energy.

You cannot separate yourself from this deep and great universal truth. You cannot live in this world and not be ultimately contributing to one or the other. Inevitably, you base your thoughts, actions, and behaviors out of one or the other. Your baseline is either inherently rooted in fear and all of the resulting defenses that come from that, or rooted in love, where you are centered in the heart and you are not in a defensive posture toward the world. Which one do you truly come from? Now, don't be too quick to answer. We all know which one we truly want to come from, but that doesn't mean we really are. Don't be too quick to answer or you will short-change yourself. Then you will be short on change!

Any form of self-reproach, any inner anger, any negative emotions that result in negative judgment toward your self is a mini-war against self. Anything that is not rooted in self-love is a war against self. I know these words are strong, but we cannot, as a world culture, risk self-denial any longer. Our ultimate accountability is the accountability to our soul lessons and their personal resolution. For, if we deny the healing of our self, we deny the healing of our planet, as our ripples move outward from self to relationship with others, our work environments, communities, states, and countries.

Don't miss the opportunity and essential necessity to truly connect with your God-given, divine, loving self. To do this, you must be fearlessly honest with yourself and courageously self-accountable. Your divine, loving self is your birth identity, and is truly who you are. Self-honesty and self-accountability are your ultimate responsibilities and are the only way to truly heal this world and this planet.

Remember the ripple. Be fully responsible for the ripple. It is your ripple and you are responsible for it—no one else. Take care of your ripple. Love yourself and heal the world. There is no separation. If we all lived from this space of love in every moment of our lives, these seemingly independent love-infused ripples would actually create a divine God-effect on earth. Oh, how we are all so intrinsically connected!

Can you begin to feel the illusion of separation that is not real? In this illusion of our separate, ego-based selves—exuding anger, indignant feelings, judgment, and attempts to control one another—we would create a collective tsunami effect and ultimately obliterate our beloved selves, and possibly our beloved planet, right out of existence.

Do you get the critical importance of this? Consider that the spiritual and physical aspects of us are intrinsically connected. This would then be the key to our survival on earth. The divine oneness that we truly are cannot exist in a state of separation because it is not separation. It would have to explode out of existence and disintegrate because it cannot live indefinitely in denial of itself. Its only hope, then, would be deconstruction until it could find a way to reassemble anew—perhaps as another planet in another time.

This is what the energy of war perpetuates, what nuclear war would actualize. We think of nuclear war as being derived from the splitting of the atom, when the "war" aspect is actually a splitting of ourselves. Each and every one of us creates the ripples that determine our collective thriving. It is our ultimate responsibility to be accountable for the ripples we choose to send out. In this sense, we are guardians of ourselves, each other, and ultimately our beloved earth!

Be brave; step up to your divine true self and know that I love you. Reach for this in yourself. It is your yearning! Love yourself! Don't get lost in shame or self-reproach. As you read these words, if it is stirring mistakes you have made along the way, if it is causing you to see your not so pretty side, do not get mad at yourself. You would then be coming from self-loathing and self-anger; that would be your ripple. Your ripple would then begin as a war within yourself. Don't be so quick to say that there are no wars within you. That would only be fear blocking your responsibility. Know that you are big enough and beautiful enough to handle this sacred task; that is why you are here!

Remember, you are here to be a guardian to yourself, one

another, and our beloved earth. Ignite this ultimate truth of who you are from deep within your soul, for deep within your soul, you already know this to be true. Awaken the sleeping beauty within your heart.

Chapter Four

Earth School, Duality, and the Lie of Self-Defectiveness

There is no separation. Let's explore this further. Our experience of "separation" is an illusion, the grand illusion of the false, fear-based self. Think about this. We live in a world where we must experience opposites. Why is this? Because to know love in its fullest possible knowing, we must know its opposite, fear. Negative emotion is always driven by fear, and judgment which comes out of fear, is always driven by a sense of inadequacy, be it conscious or unconscious. They are based out of the illusion of a separate, not-God-connected self. We learn and eventually re-experience our essence by falling from our essence. To this end, we live in a world of duality. In our world of duality, we experience fear to understand love, we experience lack to understand abundance, we experience angst to understand peaceful acceptance, and we experience grief to understand joy.

This is our earthly existence; nowhere else in any other dimension do we experience duality. It is here only in our earth school. Ironically, what we came here to find out is that duality is actually an illusion. We experience ourselves in an illusion of separateness from others and are vague and unclear on the sacred truth of our oneness. When we resolve duality, we recognize the oneness in everything and everyone, the sameness. What is this sameness, you ask? It is the sameness of divine love. The more we connect with that, the more we realize the illusion, the made-up game of everything else that we play with, get caught with, mad at, and indignant. There is no separation within our inner being or between each other. All is truly one.

Remember, most of us are not brought up in our lives with a true sense of empowerment and self-love. We are taught to diminish ourselves. Somewhere in those early years of life, we get shifted out of this original natural state. This is usually very early, and is the beginning of shame that feeds the fear-based small self. Duality is birthed out of this small self. As such, it is no more real than the false, fear-based self. Both represent the illusion we are here to resolve.

I have learned that it truly helps to name our distracted voice that is vulnerable to the fear-based small self. I like to call it the "monkey brain," collectively. We all have this monkey brain. It is not grounded in the heart; it is playing with itself—in its own head! Yes, it is a *head game*. It is not real. It is self-contained, small, and a pseudo-universe unto itself. My personal name for this ruminating, mind-chattering voice is "Blah-blah." It allows me to be playful at catching myself when my mind chatter tries to take over my heart truths and throw me off, like a little robber trying to make way with what does not belong to her. What would you name your "monkey"? You can use this name to lovingly redirect yourself back to your heart.

Whenever you catch yourself in negativity, you can also take a breathing time-out. You can take a few slower, deeper breaths when doing this. Remember, conscious breaths are always grounding: they get you out of your head and into the rest of your body. This creates an easier path to your heart center. So, you will hear me say often to take a few breaths. This is simple, powerful, and should not be overlooked. Think about it: when you sigh, doesn't that result in a more comfortable and relaxed feeling? That's because when you sigh, you are releasing emotional holds that had you captivated by the mind-chattering robber. Yes, all that in a sigh. We don't sigh when we are already relaxed and released.

So, with each breath, you get softer, your objections quiet down, and your judgments begin to surrender. Take a few breaths now. Can you feel your self-acceptance and acceptance of others returning again as you do this? Can you feel your mind quieting and a sense of serenity returning? Take a few more breathes if you need to. Don't rush, please! You spent a lifetime getting to this point. You deserve to breathe. Bree-aathe.... it will truly connect you back to your spirit and your heart.

Why has it been so difficult to accept this beautiful truth of who we are, divine and always God-connected? Why has it been so difficult to live within this truth and express it outwardly, into our lives? We lie to ourselves every day, and most of the time we don't even know it. Why? The ego wants to defend itself; it doesn't want annihilation. The ego is the false self, the self that is created to protect us from our fears and insecurities.

When we were children, most of us were taught some aspect of shame. The "spilt-milk" syndrome, which I will call it, comes in many forms, but the concluding line that is delivered to the child is always the same: "You are bad, you bad boy (or girl). You should not have done that." Whatever "that" is, doesn't matter. What matters is that it is tied to the self with the suggestion that our very selves are defective.

That is the biggest lie ever told to humankind, bigger than Santa Claus—at least with Santa Claus, the adults know it is not true and eventually the children learn the truth. But with the lie of self-defectiveness, no one really knows it is not true! Even some of our great religions perpetuate that we are born in sin and need to be forgiven. We need only to forgive ourselves. We need to return to self-love.

And here is the key—the true big key. By refusing to accept the lie that we are defective any longer, we begin the journey of reclaiming our God-created, divine, beautiful selves, ending the denial of our true essence. We are created in the image of God. We, in fact, are a "fractal" of God.[3] And so we must begin the journey home because, somehow, most of us have fallen from this divine grace. The negative self-judgments that have perpetuated shame have put this entire lie into play.

You see, many people are truly afraid to own their "stuff" and become accountable. Why is that? The simple answer is that this is unconsciously tied to shame. For so many of us, when we admit a mistake, we automatically and unconsciously internalize, "I am a bad person." This was triggered from the first time we ever felt that way. That original feeling of "I am a bad person" is so painful that we unconsciously guard against that feeling like death itself. So we don't own our stuff because we don't want to feel defective.

The direct implication for self-healing, and the self-loving way to handle these moments, is instead to reach a place within our hearts where we acknowledge our mistakes but not tie them to feelings of unworthiness. Then we would be coming from self-acceptance and could easily say, "Okay, I made a mistake. What can I learn from this? Have I hurt anyone? Do I need to acknowledge anyone?" Ultimately, in this example, we do not feel defective and are not afraid to own our stuff.

This is what the healing of the "spilt-milk" syndrome is all about: a return to the love of the self and the willingness to take personal accountability without shame. We then confront what we need to confront within ourselves—our personal ripples and their related emotions for which we must be accountable—all from a place of self-acceptance and self-love. This is the path to self-honoring, honoring of others, the removal of self-denial, and the healing of the lie of self-defectiveness.

Chapter Five

Our Energy Centers and Balancing

Let's look closely at the word "emotion" and break it down this way: *e-motion*. Based on the Latin word *emovere*, *e* means "out" and *movere* means "move." I interpret that to mean our emotions are meant to be in natural state of "motion," and are meant to move "out" of us. In order for this to happen, we must live from a state of observation where we do not become fixated in judgment or hooked on a belief—something we have explored in the previous chapters. I also refer to the "e" in "emotion" as symbolic for "energy," since everything in the universe is ultimately energy. So "emotion" is "energy in motion" in its most balanced, unrepressed, and not over-exerted state. In addition to our emotions having a chemical basis, our emotions also have an electromagnetic basis producing energetic vibrations. Needless to say, our fear-based emotions produce an energy vibration that is different than our love-based emotions. Let me explain further:

Some of you may be aware of the experimentation on water molecules by Dr. Masaru Emoto. He has written several books depicting his discoveries including *The Hidden Messages in Water* (Simon & Shuster, 2005). Dr. Emoto is a doctor of alternative medicine who was able to show us the profound effect of our emotions on water molecules. He did this over many studies where water crystals were exposed to different focused intentions through words, images, and music to convey a range of emotional energy. The same water molecules seemed to "change expression" as they were exposed to these differences. He captured, with microphotography, photographs of these water crystals. Exposed to loving words, beautiful images, or harmonious music, they formed brilliant, complex, and colorful snowflake patterns. In contrast, water exposed to negative thoughts or pollution formed incomplete, asymmetrical patterns with dull colors.

What a truly powerful indication of how profoundly our thoughts and feelings affect physical reality. Remember, our bodies are over 50 percent water and the earth body we live on is 50 percent water also. Ripple away, but with conscious loving care!

Paralleling Dr. Emoto's work, ongoing research at the Institute of HeartMath, summarized on their website, *www.heartmath. org*, has demonstrated that negative emotions produce erratic and disordered patterns in heart rhythm, and positive emotions produce smooth and coherent patterns in heart rhythm.[4] The Institute's research has also revealed that the heart generates the most powerful known electromagnetic field. In comparison to the brain, the heart's field is sixty times greater in amplitude and affects every cell of the body. Other bodily rhythms have been shown to naturally synchronize to the heart's rhythmic frequency during sustained feelings of love and appreciation. Experiments at the Institute have also shown that the heart's electromagnetic field can transmit information below the conscious level between people, and that one person's brain waves can synchronize to another person's heartbeat.

So, through our ripples of thoughts infused by the emotions of our hearts, we send out different vibrational frequencies that directly impact and influence each other. Which frequency do you want to send out into our collective experiences?

Let's look at the electromagnetic vibrations of our emotional energy more deeply. *Chakras* are known as our energy centers, or centers of vibrational force, that exist within the body and serve as invisible focal points through which we receive and transmit energy.[5] It is the Sanskrit term for "wheel" or "turning" that originated in ancient Hindu texts. They have been described by many as vortex centers in the body with a rotational force, and are typically depicted as flower-like or wheel-like patterns.

One way to explain chakras is through the example of acupuncture, which utilizes the body's electromagnetic energy for healing. Whereas Western medicine deals with our chemistry, Eastern medicine deals with healing through our energy. Hence, it is called "energy" medicine. When our body's energy is healed and balanced, we are balanced on all levels: mentally, physically, emotionally, and spiritually. Our bodies are also supported in resisting or reversing diseases associated with each of the chakras. When our energy centers are in balance, we are in balance.

According to Hindu tradition, there are seven major chakras that run from the base of our spines to the tops of our heads and are located at different nerve bundles within the body. In addition, we have other subtle body chakras. Each of the chakras vibrates to different frequencies of sound and color, corresponds to different organs and glands in the body, and has different emotional meanings.[6] Let's become acquainted with each of the major chakras and their attributes. I have created a chakra chart of the seven major chakras on page 34, as well as a figure of the human body with the chakras in their corresponding locations for your reference as you read along (see page 36).

The first chakra, known as the root chakra, located at the base of the spine, vibrates to the sound of LA, and its color is red. On a physical level, it influences the sex glands, sex drive, reproduction, and is the seat of our physical life force. This chakra, on an emotional level, relates to the phrase, "I feel." It also relates to the phrase, "I am here; here I am, rooted in the earth, born. I exist." It relates to our basic needs for survival.

The second chakra, known as the spleen chakra, located three inches below the navel, vibrates to the sound of BA, and its color is orange. On a physical level, it influences the spleen, liver, pancreas, and bladder, therefore affecting metabolism, di-

Chakra Centers and Their Attributes

CHAKRA & LOCATION	COLOR	SOUND	PHYSICAL INFLUENCE	EMOTIONAL ATTRIBUTES
ROOT – base of spine	red	LA	sex glands, sex drive, reproduction	feeling, arriving, existing
SPLEEN – three inches below navel	orange	BA	spleen, liver, pancreas, bladder, metabolism, digestion, immunity, detoxification	desire, want, sexual expression
SOLAR PLEXUS – Just above navel	yellow	RA	sympathetic nervous system, adrenals, heartbeat, muscular energy, digestion, circulation	manifesting, motivating, actualizing
HEART – center of chest	emerald green	YA-MM	thymus gland, heart	unconditional love, connecting with others
THROAT – Base of throat	sky blue	HA	thyroid, balance of the nervous system	speaking one's truth, creative expression
THIRD EYE – center of forehead	indigo	AH	pituitary gland, overall endocrines	inward looking, intuitive connecting
CROWN – top of head	violet	OM	pineal gland	divine God-connection

gestion, detoxification and immunity. This chakra on an emotional level relates to the phrase, "I want, I desire." It also relates to sexual expression.

The third chakra, known as the solar plexus chakra, located just above the navel, vibrates to the sound of RA, and its color is yellow. On a physical level, it influences the sympathetic nervous system, adrenal glands, heartbeat, muscular energy, digestion, and circulation. This chakra on an emotional level is about manifesting: "I can, I make happen, I motivate, and I actualize."

The fourth chakra, known as the heart chakra, located in the center of the chest, vibrates to the two-syllable sound of YA-MM, and its color is emerald green. On a physical level, it influences the thymus gland and the heart. On an emotional level, this is where unconditional love resides. It simply says, "I love, I connect." It is also about balance, equilibrium, and our connection to others. It is the center point in the chakra system, with three chakras below and three chakras above.

The fifth chakra, known as the throat chakra, located at the base of the throat, vibrates to the sound of HA, and its color is sky blue. On a physical level, it influences the thyroid and the balance of the nervous system. On an emotional level, it is about speaking our truths, creative expression, inner identity, and expressing our true voice.

The sixth chakra, known as the brow center or "third eye," located in the center of the forehead, vibrates to the sound of AH, and its color is indigo. On a physical level, it influences the pituitary gland, the master gland, influencing the other endocrines. On an emotional level, it is about higher sensing, intuitive knowing, and telepathy. Where the throat chakra is about inner expressing, the brow chakra is about inward looking. It is how we connect with and access our intuitive self.

The seventh chakra, known as the crown chakra, located on top of the head, vibrates to the sound OM, the totality of all sounds, and its color is violet. On a physical level, it influences the pineal gland which is thought of as "the seat of the soul." On an emotional level it is about our connection with God, divine perfection, and all-knowingness. It is our connection to the divine source, the creator from which we are derived. It upholds the essences of all the other chakras and, in that sense, is the total energy signature of each individual.

I suggest a simple practice that you can engage to balance the chakras: Sit quietly and take a few deep, slow, grounding breaths. Then imagine each chakra, in its location, one by one, spinning as a ball of energy. See its color and hear its sound,

The Seven Major Chakra Centers

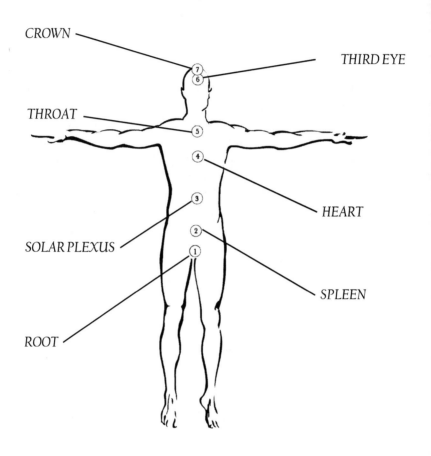

CROWN

THIRD EYE

THROAT

HEART

SOLAR PLEXUS

SPLEEN

ROOT

spending time in each one. As you imagine each one spinning, affirm to yourself that the chakra is perfectly balanced, healthy, and strong and that you are in a perfect state of balance and wellness. Trust your inner guidance on how long to stay with each chakra.

Another practice is to gently sing the sounds of each of the chakras by extending the name of their sound vibration out loud. Simply singing the sound vibrations of each chakra can be immediately balancing. For instance, for the first chakra, the root, you would sing "laaaaa," and for the second chakra, you would sing "baaaaa," and so on through the chakras. Choose tones that feel intuitively right for you when singing the name of each sound. You can also combine these two practices into one by toning aloud as you imagine each chakra spinning in its color.

Balancing our chakras not only helps us function more optimally on an emotional level, but can even help to prevent or reverse diseases and physical conditions associated with each chakra.

When our chakras are not in balance, we become under-expressive or over-expressive of the corresponding unbalanced energy of that chakra. Let's look specifically at each chakra when not in a balanced state, and what corresponding challenges and vulnerabilities may result. (The following is per the author's studied knowledge and applied interpretation:)

The root chakra, as a reminder, relates to survival, arriving, being present, and meeting our basic needs. If this chakra is not in balance, we could become selfish and greedy about grabbing up resources. We could push to get what we think we need without regard to the other. We may also feel inadequate and powerless in meeting our basic needs, causing us to feel threatened easily. On a physical level, imbalance and disease related to our sexual organs and nutrition could result.

The spleen chakra relates to want and desire. If this is not in balance, we may feel inadequate and scattered in our focus and direction. We may be out of touch with our desires and wants and have difficulty knowing what truly drives and ignites our passion for life. We may also disconnect ourselves emotionally or diminish our self-value, making ourselves small. Alternatively, we may become prone to addiction, attempting to fill our desires from the outside rather than from our true essence, from the inside. On a physical level, imbalance and disease related to metabolism, digestion, toxicity, and blood sugar could result.

The solar plexus chakra relates to manifesting, making things happen, and feeling our power in the world. If this chakra is not in balance, we may be prone to feeling powerless or we may tend to overpower and overbear on others. We may be either insecure and make ourselves feel insignificant or we may be controlling, forceful, ruthless, and insensitive to others as we become self-absorbed and self-centered. On a physical level, imbalance and disease related to stress, such as ulcers, nervous disorders, and fatigue may result.

The heart chakra relates to our ability to love and form meaningful connections. When this chakra is not in balance, we may be fearful of emotional intimacy, become isolated, and have challenges with trust. Alternatively, we may be challenged with anger or unconsciously sabotage our relationships. On a physical level, imbalance and disease related to immunity, heart vulnerability, and circulation could result.

The throat chakra relates to communication. When this is not in balance, we are prone to not expressing our voice, being meek in our communication, and holding ourselves back in assertiveness. Alternatively, we may over-communicate, possibly becoming blunt or plowing over other's feelings. On a physical level, imbalance and disease related to the nervous system, metabolism, the throat, and our muscular system could result.

The third eye chakra relates to our intuition and higher knowing. When this is not in balance, we may be prone to operating only out of our lower chakras, becoming lost in our small self's ego, manipulating others, and not following our higher wisdom. On a physical level, imbalance and disease related to the endocrine system or the brain could result.

The crown chakra relates to our God-connectedness, and when this one is out of balance we may feel lost in the world and cut off from our true divine essence. Just as is true of the third eye chakra, we may also be more prone to operating only out of our lower chakras, becoming lost in a delusional and ego-driven sense of self. On a physical level, imbalance and disease related to cognition may result.

When you feel unbalanced in your life, think specifically regarding what that imbalance represents. In other words, what life area or emotional, mental, or physical state does not feel balanced? Getting in touch with this can help you know what chakras are out of balance. By doing further meditation and balancing work on these chakras, you will support the related aspects of yourself and your life to flow more easily.

Chapter Six

Grounding Love in the Heart

A dear friend, Nadine Miller, who has been a sister and a guiding light in my life, once said to me, "If you never read another book, if you never read another word of inspiration, just always come from the heart no matter what you do, and you will never need to know another thing." Her words are powerful, essential, and true.

We must learn to ground ourselves and live in a balanced manner through love in the heart. It then becomes much easier to dispel the illusion and deception of the fear-based, ego-driven, small self. The most essential soul lesson for all of us to truly understand and integrate is to navigate in life through the heart. We must navigate our personal relationship to ourselves and others through the heart on all levels—mentally, physically, emotionally, and spiritually.

I recently learned that the heart vibrates at a frequency of 528Hz and produces the third note, "MI." This is known as a *divine frequency* and is part of other divine frequencies, known as Solfeggio tones that create changes in our energy patterns, according to Dr. Leonard Horowitz in his book, *Healing Codes for the Biological Apocalypse.*[7] These original sound frequencies were used in Gregorian chants, and were believed to create tremendous spiritual blessings when sung in harmony. According to Dr. Horowitz, the heart frequency is said to be the energy of the highest form of spiritual love and is the tone of transformation and miracles. The third note, MI, originates from the phrase *mira gestorum* in Latin meaning "miracle." Strikingly, Dr. Horowitz explains, this is the exact frequency used by genetic biochemists to repair broken DNA—our very genetic blueprint!

I will share with you a guided meditation on grounding love in the heart that I recently learned from another friend, Susan Hanson, during a crystal healing weekend in Santa Fe. To set the stage for this meditation, Susan explained that our lower chakras are about survival and that they need to be grounded in the heart chakra. After this happens and as we ascend to the heart level with the emotions created and held within the first three chakras, our love becomes compassionate and vibrates easily to the heart color, emerald green.

Right above our heart chakra is the higher heart chakra; its color is fuchsia. This is one of the subtle body chakras that vibrate in half-tones and function like a bridge to higher levels of understanding.[8] Susan explained that the higher heart chakra needs to be tied in to our main heart chakra. The heart chakra and the higher heart chakra together become the gateway to living in higher love-based consciousness.

Susan further explained that our throat and third eye chakras also need to be brought into the heart chakra, to bring unconditional love into our communications, expressions, and connections. The only one that doesn't need to be brought into the heart chakra is the crown chakra because it is already connected in divine loving perfection.

To do this meditation, please refer to the box entitled, "Grounding Love in the Heart," on the next page. Alternatively, for your ease of meditating, each of the guided meditations in this book is available as an audio download on my website, *www.ultimate-healing.com.*

GROUNDING LOVE IN THE HEART

First, close your eyes and get into a comfortable position, either sitting or lying down. Breathe in and imagine a bright green ball of light at the level of your heart. Take a few deep breaths in and out, slower than usual, while continuing to imagine this ball of radiant, bright green light.

Remain aware of this vibrant green ball of light in the heart chakra, and now imagine a ball of radiant red light in the root chakra. Breathe in this red ball of light; bring it into existence and really see it, as you continue to breathe slower and deeper than usual. Now imagine a figure eight connecting it to the heart chakra and the heart's radiant green ball of light. Breathe this in a few times slowly and deeply.

Next, move your attention to just under the navel and imagine a radiant ball of orange light. Breathe this in a few times as you imagine this ball of radiant orange light. Now imagine a figure eight connecting it to the heart chakra and its radiant green ball of light. Breathe this in a few times slowly and deeply.

When you are ready, imagine a ball of radiant yellow light in the solar plexus and breathe this in a few times. Now, imagine a figure eight connecting it to the radiant green ball of light in the heart chakra. Take your time, allowing your breathing to continue slowly and deeper than usual.

Next, imagine the fuchsia color of the higher heart chakra and see a radiant bright fuchsia ball of light, and breathe this image of fuchsia light in a few times. Tie a figure eight from the higher heart chakra to the immediate heart chakra and its radiant green light. Breathe slowly and deeply and be present with this.

Now, imagine a ball of radiant, sky blue light at the throat chakra and breathe this in a few times. Next, imagine a figure eight connecting it to the heart chakra and its green radiant ball of light. Breathe slowly and deeply and be present with this.

Lastly, imagine a ball of radiant indigo light at the third eye chakra and breathe this in a few times. Imagine a figure eight connecting it to the radiant green ball of light in the heart chakra.

Now, just be still and breathe peacefully, experiencing your chakras grounded in the heart.

After you complete the meditation, notice what you are feeling and how you feel now compared to before you began this meditation. By doing this meditation repeatedly, you will be able to live and relate from your heart center much more easily.

It is so very important to truly navigate all of your relationships, expressions, and actions in life through the divine loving energy of the heart. It will transform everything you say and do into the vibrational energy of love. There is no better way to completely heal both your inner and outer worlds. Can you feel this? That is your heart waking up. That is your heart beating in love as it was intended to do. Welcome home, my friend!

You see, you never really got lost all of the way. You would not even be reading these words if you did. This book would not have appealed to you. Most importantly, you would not be feeling what you are feeling now had you gotten completely lost. Distracted? Yes. Thrown off balance? Yes. Knocked around a bit? Yes. Can you forgive yourself? You are not at fault. Take a deep, deeeeep breath now. Take it in. Take *you* in. Get reacquainted with your true God-given self now. And thank yourself for your willingness to let go of the "old hat" and arrive. Bless your heart and your soul, you beautiful human being! You are the light you have been looking for! Now breathe some more. Feel this. Be the love you have been looking for.

The next time you go out into the world and make eye contact with people, try a simple shift. As you see through your eyes, gaze through your heart. It helps to take some conscious deeper breaths as you allow yourself to feel this shift in your gaze. Practice this now. Do you feel your heart opening and expanding? Even in just imagining this shift, you may notice that you become more focused in the moment and that your thoughts become quieter as your heart wakes up. Become aware of what it feels like to view and experience the world through your heart. Go into your day and practice this. When you do this, ask yourself as you look back on this experience, are you falling in love again? What do you feel? Is your heart softening? Have your previous attachments to judgments weakened, maybe even disappeared?

It is okay to let tears flow, as you may feel that you've come home to a place from which you did not even realize you had strayed. It is not your fault, however disconnected or lost you became. There is no fault in divinity. Remember, we have already established that you are divine. We may make mistakes, but there is no fault. A mistake is a *missed take*, not a reason to hold ourselves in an emotional prison. Can you accept your mistakes? They are simply guideposts toward ultimate balancing and self-love.

I invite you now to read one of the most beautiful and powerful poems to which I have strongly and deeply related. This is a poem about loving ourselves enough to live in full expression of ourselves. It was written by Marianne Williamson and is entitled, "Our Deepest Fear." Read this poem slowly and allow it to resonate deeply within your heart center as you breathe in its clear wisdom:

Our deepest fear is not that we are inadequate.

Our deepest fear is that we are powerful beyond measure.

It is our light, not our darkness, that most frightens us.

We ask ourselves, who am I to be brilliant, gorgeous, talented, fabulous?

Actually, who are you not to be?

You are a child of God.

Your playing small doesn't serve the world.

There's nothing enlightened about shrinking so that other people won't feel insecure around you.

We are all meant to shine, as children do.

We were born to make manifest the glory of God that is within us.

It's not just in some of us; it's in everyone.

And as we let our own light shine,

we unconsciously give other people permission to do the same.

As we're liberated from our fear, our presence automatically liberates others.[9]

Did this deeply inspiring poem stir your heart? Are you sitting more within your heart now? Here is another poem. This one is about returning over and over, without shame, to that sacred place, when we become estranged. It is by the thirteenth-century Sufi mystic, Jalal ad-Din Muhammad, a timeless poet who has expressed humanity's essence and soul lessons many times through his writing:

Come, come, whoever you are.

Wanderer, worshipper, lover of leaving—it doesn't matter,

Ours is not a caravan of despair.

Even if you have broken your vows a thousand times,

Come, yet again, come.[10]

Remember, in this earth school we learn and re-experience our essence by falling from our essence. What is our essence? That which is essential! There is only one thing that is essential. Yes, you guessed it: it is love. Again, let's begin today making it a practice to come from the heart. Ground yourself through love in your heart center and your life will instantaneously become more fulfilling—literally the second you begin doing this. Yes, your personal transformation can begin or deepen instantaneously. The act of it is really that easy. It is the choosing that becomes so difficult. Why? Why would choosing such a beautiful thing be so difficult?

Chapter Seven

Getting Lost Along the Way

Imagine a very beautiful and unconditional love-connected being, not yet here on earth but destined to be here and is on her way. We will name her Clarity. Clarity resides in a most sacred and supportive holding environment as she makes her way inter-dimensionally toward earth. Clarity moves as a pure light-body through a sacred tunnel into a light she has never known and she arrives on earth. She is utterly and totally connected to God when she arrives. You might say she even is God—well, at least a perfect holographic imprint of God.

Feel her, because you are her. You are Clarity. She is your birth self. She is physical, beautiful, unstained, pure, clear, receptive, trusting, open, vibrant, and full of love. Her eyes reflect God. There is a quiet about her. She has no judgment; she just is. Have you ever connected with the eyes of a newborn? They are portals through which you can reconnect with God, and your true nature.

Clarity moves about life in that first year not able to talk, acclimating and quietly taking in this new and strange world around her. Hmm, she is loved day to day, but then there is this strange, out-of-tune, disharmonious vibration. "What is that noise?" Her parents are arguing and yelling. The vibration shouts through her and makes her feel very, very uncomfortable. They don't even know it. In fact, they may even think, "Oh our baby, Clarity, won't be affected; she cannot even understand the words."

Ahhh, but they are so wrong. Clarity, in fact, understands the words more than they do. What she understands is that their vibration is disharmonious. This confuses her because these are the people that take care of her. So her brain gets a little jostled around and separated from her heart.

Of course, not everyone has had yelling, arguing parents. There are other disharmonious vibrations. For instance, we covered one earlier—a very significant one—the "spilt-milk" syndrome, resulting in the internalization of "I'm a bad boy" or "I'm a bad girl." Wow, what a sad and negative reverberation, shooting through such a beautiful spirit. Can you feel the stain? When did someone tell you that you were bad as a child? Rather, it was your behavior that was bad, which had nothing to do with the beautiful child you were.

When we came to earth in our original God-created state as Clarity, our essence was like crystal-clear water with a full spectrum of vibrant colors in our sacred reflection. The first disharmonious reverberation came, like a spill of murky crude oil seeping into our spectacular water essence. Okay, maybe just a little spill; it will get absorbed, right? And then another, and another, and another. Can you feel how even one oil spill spreads so readily through clear water?

Anytime in childhood that we were shamed, made to feel bad for whom we were as a result of a mistaken action—or, even worse, when we made no mistake at all—our beautiful essence received a spill. As children dependent upon the adult world, typically we accepted these false accusations, and became "stained" with this disharmonious oil.

You get the picture, right? Kind of "crude," huh? This is how we, as Clarity, got stained little by little, and how we lost touch with our essence. In fact we began to confuse these stains with who we really are, because it is what we began to know. Clarity began to lose *clarity*!

Does it sound like I am exaggerating a bit? Really? Give it

some thought. Do you love yourself? We must return to our true divine nature for our ultimate healing. Clarity, in her remembered state, knows. Can you meet her again? It is time; the world needs you, you need you, and I need you.

Dr. Emoto's experiments with water serve as a powerful example of what happened to Clarity's essence of pure, crystalline water depending on the emotional vibrations she was exposed to. The degree of oil stains from disharmonious, shame-based messages of our early childhood experiences account for the degree of confusion in our spirits. The extent of these toxic, negative messages closely equals the extent that we may become afraid to face our lessons of personal growth. This is because the embedded negative energy of shame causes a false belief of "defectiveness." They are our earliest experiences of negative emotional energy states that are contradictory to our essential, true, divinely perfect selves.

Since these energies are based out of illusion and the false self of others, they confuse Clarity. She begins to confuse this state of illusion as her true self. So, gradually, in those first few ever-so-precious formative years of life, little by little we fall from the highest form of grace—from where we came.

What does this really mean to fall from grace? In biblical terms, it refers to falling from a state of God-obedience toward a state of disobedience. As a deeper way of understanding this: we become disobedient to our God-connected selves and instead obedient to the illusion of our small, fear-based, ego-deceived selves. After all, we are a holographic image of God; we are just in a forgotten state of godliness.

Yes, I know this can cause you to feel very sad. But, it is so very important to take that sadness and funnel it through compassion. If you funnel it through anger, blame of others, or blame of yourself, you are not yourself again. Remember, this is because the essence of your *self* is unconditional love. In anger, you would then have lost *clarity* again. Clarity wants to be rediscovered, nurtured, cradled, and cleared of her accumulated oil well of confusion. Embrace Clarity. You are Clarity. We were all Clarity as we arrived on earth and took on our physical form. It is your true first name before you were given your earthly name. Now it is time to return to her state of pure knowing.

Before the writer's retreat in Sedona, Arizona, I experienced a metaphor for what we are talking about here. I was participating in the last of our preparatory conference webinar calls before the retreat. On this day, I was hiking through an area named the "Cowpies" and headed to the top of "Mitten Ridge." Atop the ridge, I breathed into my spirit the serene beauty, recognizing Mother Earth's nature and her divinely perfected state of self-love. Nature does not get mad at herself or self-deprecate, does she? That is not natural. That is not Mother Nature's nature! It is clearly not our nature, either. We have been living so unnaturally. She is a tremendous example for all of us.

Realizing I would not make it down from the ridge before the webinar call, I hiked down a little to get out of the wind and find a rock outcrop to sit on. The call began; cell phone reception was with me. Victoria, a holistic practitioner and member of our writing group, guided us through Resonance Repatterning, a method for resolving emotional energy constrictions and unconscious patterns that limit us. We named our fear-based thoughts that had been resonating with us and then connected with the affirming positive empowering statements with which we did not yet resonate. She re-patterned us through singing different tones. Remember that when we sing tones that resonate with our chakras, this has an instant balancing effect. I felt good.

The call was not over, but I decided to start walking and making my way down as I continued to listen. She had Tom, our writing retreat leader, repeat the sentences for all of us to make sure the re-patterning had succeeded and completed. She then measured the success through a process called muscle testing (I will explain this later).

While I was listening, I became lost and could not regain my bearings as to whether I was above or below the ridge trail. Moderate concern crept in. Then, as I was working on staying out of fear and in a grounded place internally, I spotted some people, maybe seventy-five to one hundred feet below me. I yelled down, "Hey, is that the trail down there?" They yelled up an affirming "yes." Acknowledging them as my "trail angels," I made my way down as they kindly waited for me.

I thanked them and said, "It's really easy to get lost up there." One of them responded, "You were not lost; you were just navigating." It was practically poetic because all of this was happening while Tom was repeating the re-patterned sentences back to Victoria for the group, as we "navigated" through fear back to our natural, love-connected states. It was like layers of a beautiful life song. The tones of nature stirred me ever so deeply. My heart was so open that a butterfly flew out! I was in love.

So, yes, this life is a journey in which we begin in love, then navigate our way through fear, only to return to the heart and our true, God-created, essential selves. Remember these words and let them be a guidepost for your journey. Know that this is where you are going, and it will all make sense! I wrote a poem once that celebrated this releasing of fear and the re-opening of the heart that I will share now. It is entitled, "The Trickster":

The Trickster came often,
and wrapped its deceiving ego turban
tight and bound around
my mind now plagued.

I became a crescent-woven, unbaked caterpillar
desperately trying not to lose
my guts, as all I thought I ever was died.

One day, the turban spilled open
like the tongue of a serpent.
Out flew an eagle,
and she danced and played
to the bronze god sun.

And seven rain beams,

birthed out of compassionate tears,

eyed back and danced to the eagle

the likeness of her God-portrayed freedom.

We never lose our way altogether; it can just feel that way when we are navigating. Perhaps we lose the forest through the trees, but there is always, always a way back.

Here is another story I experienced in nature: a story of a tree. It is a story that illustrates an internal self-correcting mechanism that we all have. It insists we find our way back, the way that isn't rooted in ego and fear. The beacon of light of our true self says, "Come back to me, I love you, I love you." So, on this particular day, I was walking along a beautiful wooded path in Hagerstown, Maryland, an oasis of a lovely city park. In these beautiful surroundings, I came upon a tree that was noticeably different from the others. It started out growing maybe seven feet or so and, all of a sudden, it made a left turn and started growing perfectly sideways. After doing that for a good five to six feet, it suddenly grew straight up again!

I once told this tree story to a client, and she simply and perfectly summarized the lesson in it: "You cannot grow sideways." At least we cannot effectively grow sideways—that is, do we ever want to? Who wants the chiropractic bill to remedy that! We all have an inner self-corrective mechanism that is connected in the heart and wants our wholeness and our wellness. Actually, through life, we make our mistakes as a means to reconnect to our true selves, because every time we do that we build our strength toward wholeness until we fully return. These are the lessons of duality returning us to our divine source.

Can you forgive yourself yet? On a more essential level, anyway, there is nothing to forgive, because you were never defective. Can you release yourself into self-acceptance? Are you ready to free yourself from your prison of self-condemnation? If you can truly say, "I love myself" and feel this with all of your heart and soul, I congratulate you and I honor you. If you cannot say "I love you" to yourself and feel it with no blocks whatsoever, then you have aspects of self-condemnation to resolve. And I love you; I honor you, and encourage you to read on! You are beautiful, and you are a spiritual warrior consciously ready to do the work of the soul.

To those who would not pick up a book like this, who may be completely unconscious of their "stuff" and are busy acting out in the world and denying their emotional self-responsibility, let us love them and honor their path. Even unconscious navigating is beautiful, because still deep inside of them, Clarity, like a beacon of light, patiently waits for their return home, even when they don't know it. To those of them who are directly hurting others along the way, let us feel compassion for them and send them a prayer of healing. In fact, the more you connect with your heart, the more you will naturally want to do this for them. Can you imagine the power of healing in this world as we all come from this compassionate state, being grounded in the heart?

Yes, you will continue to get lost and have to find yourself again. This is the nature of our healing and return to love where we learn to live a conscious and intentional life.

I will compare our emotional evolution with weight training at the gym. When we first work a muscle it says, "Ouch, I like me the way I am. Please leave me alone. That hurts." Similarly, when we are learning to stay grounded in love through the heart, this emotional "muscle" first says, "Ouch, I like my old way. I am justified in my old way. Here is my artillery of reasons to protect my fortress of fear and why I need to stay this way. Thank you very much, but this is not for me."

Whoa....but what happens when we instead build this emotional "muscle" with perseverance, one repetition at a time? Yes, yes, we become stronger and then we actually desire the new feeling this brings. The fear-based self does not know that we actually feel so much better in this new strong place and that we want more of what feels so much better. And so we evolve our spirits one repetition at a time with loving patience.

Through patience, self-compassion, and perseverance, we love ourselves along the way. Certainly, we cannot get to greater self-love through self-deprecation and demeaning ourselves. Do you see the beauty in this? We must love ourselves through our unloving states! Now that is a joyful twist, isn't it? We are the answer we have been looking for! We must love ourselves through building this emotional muscle in all of its growing pains. And we must keep going back; it is through this repetition and the gift of self-patience and loving perseverance that we are able to seat ourselves more firmly in the heart.

Sure, we will make excuses along the way. When we don't take true self-responsibility, we are in effect proclaiming, "I don't want to work out today; I am tired." Fear-based thoughts and feelings of inadequacy say, "The world has beaten me down; that one was too much." Or, "Yeah, but he or she really hurt me. I am allowed to hold onto that one. I don't want to surrender my anger and righteous indignation toward 'so-and-so' today because I am justified. I want 'so-and-so' to change so I don't have to do my work of the soul." As we stay lost in self-justification, we convince ourselves that the ego, from which our false, scared, small selves are derived, is the real deal, the true self.

Do you want to be connected to your small self, which is no real connection at all and will keep you lost and out of love for as long as you allow, or do you want to go for your true divine self, not the false one, and fall in love again? The true divine self is your God-given birthright, for God gave you to you. So, when you get lost along the way, do not hold yourself in contempt, hold yourself in love.

In my teen years I wrote a poem entitled, "The Fisherman." I may not have understood at the time what the poem was really about, but many years and layers of life later the symbolism became clear. This poem is about losing our way to our true divine selves and the unconscious fear of the loss of the ego and small fear-based self:

What happens to the curious man
who probes in dungeon's gloom
on a guideless, fearless journey

to retrieve his memory loss?

He boards a dreary lonely ship—
its name, The Forgotten Room—
and navigates as guided by chance
a blinded man and boss.

He probes and searches relentlessly
upsets and overtires
yearning for a hearty catch
his mind the captive bait.

Careful not to fish too deeply
where he himself expires,
he shuns the callings of the heart,
his self-inflicted mortal fate.

So we have fallen into amnesia and this is a journey of re-membering. We must return to the heart to fall in love again and to remember who we truly are. Most of us have heard the quote, "Home is where the heart is." We are not "at home" in the truest sense unless we reside in the heart. We live in a for-gotten state or "room," yearning to "catch" our hearts, but bait-ing with our minds. Should we listen to our hearts, we would only lose the false fear-based self and escape this mortal fate.

Chapter Eight

Original Addiction

So why would we stay in fear and self-justification rather than grow into the higher and beautiful perspective of our loving selves? What is the driving force behind this emotional prison from which we refuse to set ourselves free or even notice or acknowledge that we are not free to begin with? The answer is addiction! I do not mean addiction to alcohol, drugs or other commonly known addictions; I mean "thought" addiction, and this epidemic of thought addiction that is running rampant in our world leads to tremendous emotional distortions in who we are. This then gets projected into the world around us as we spread this *dis*-ease! The root of all addiction is the same: the disconnection from the true self. Ego-based thought addiction is the "original addiction." All other addiction is secondary.

My first spiritual teacher, Peter Bloch, once shared his definition of addiction with me: "The inability to be at peace with ourselves even in our own solitude." I would shift this a bit and say that this is not a direct definition of addiction. It is what leads us into addiction because, if we cannot be at peace in our own solitude, then we are vulnerable to filling the emptiness within from the outside with external satisfactions. This fulfillment, being superficial, will not last and perpetuates a repetitious pattern. It would be like trying to fill a cup with a hole. It will never fill because the hole has to be filled with what it is truly made of and not the "substance" being put into it.

In that state, what we want is pure, but the way we go about it is destructive to ourselves and often the people who love us. Our intentions are simple and good: the desire for peace, relief, comfort, to be free of isolation, to feel good, and to feel in control. But, of course, if we fill these needs and desires from external sources, we have to keep going back for more. This is because we are not filling from the essence of our divine essential selves, the only self that is true.

The small addicted self runs out of the "substance" and must go back for more. The more we repeat this reverse workout, which is equal to the worst and most toxic junk food for the soul, the more we lose our way back to our true godly source and who we really are. In original addiction, we make our thoughts the god. In secondary addictions, we make the object of that addiction the god: in substance abuse, we make the substance the god; in gambling addiction, we make the adrenaline and endorphin release the god; in shopping addiction, we make the purchased items the god; in sex addiction, we make sex the god.

This little false god gives us superficially the things we desire or need, but at what price? It robs our souls. It comes in the dark like a trickster, a con artist with empty promises of fulfilling our needs. On some level we know this con artist lies but, coming from a disempowered self, we believe it enough to get lost in its energy: "Just this one time. I really, really need relief. I know true relief won't really come this way but, oh my God, that true way feels so difficult and out of reach, so just this one time I will go for easy quick relief. I deserve it; I hurt soooo badly. I promise to work harder to do it right the next time."

Some of you will relate to all of this because you have moved through secondary addiction or maybe still are, or are just beginning to peek through your fear. I am a recovering gambling addict. I have learned personally, from the powerful soul lessons that have come from gambling addiction, how extremely powerful addiction is—all addiction.

But what about the rest of you who may by now be feeling, "Wow, I'm so fortunate, because I never got lost in addiction." Remember, folks, none of us are exempt; we are all addicted! As long as we identify with our small self and ego-based thoughts, then yes, we are addicted. We are lost in a state of small self and we are hooked on self-justifying thoughts that keep us in this energy. We are afraid and are seeking relief from the outside in. We are not at peace with each other or with ourselves even in our own solitude.

To that end we are thought addicts, and this in fact is a very insidious addiction. If most of us have it, who is going to call us on it? Who is going to call us on an addiction that almost all of us have gotten lost in at least some of the time—if not most of the time? We get hooked on our thoughts as if they are "the truth" rather than our "personal truth," which is born out of personal life experiences and all of our accompanying distortions and defenses. Nonetheless, it would be our best shot at our personal truth, to say the most, but nothing more than that.

Okay, don't back out on me yet! How many times have you expressed your feelings to someone when you were in conflict and they barked at you or you at them with, "That's not true, that's not what happened." Any time you have gotten into one of those ball games with someone, chances are nothing either of you are stating as true is really true—not yours and not theirs. Why do we remember the same event differently when we were both in that same conversation together even one hour ago? It is because the memory we have of an event tends to start at the point of our emotional responses. Since we are addicted to our ego-based thoughts and their ensuing emotions, each person will say it began at a different point because our emotional responses began at a different point. We take the event emotionally in different ways because our emotional needs in the moment are different.

This by itself would not be so much of a problem; however, we get attached to the thoughts that support our emotional needs in a way that wants the world around us to change. We do this, rather than stepping fully into our own selves and dealing with our own responses. We are lost in our own illusions of smallness and instead focused on where we see others acting small and where we want them to change. We don't realize that the very act of wanting them to change is a reflection of our own selves caught in our own smallness. In this state of illusion, we even defend our beliefs at times as if our very lives were dependent on them.

So the "substance" is actually the "ego," and we attempt to fill ourselves with it to feel relief, pleasure, and other emotional responses. These are the same things that traditional addicts want. There is no difference. The more we try to fill from the ego-based small self, the more we have to go back for more. The more we do this, the further we get from our true, divine source. In other words, we are addicted to our small false selves. We are addicted to the thoughts that support the small self's survival. It is fear-based because it fears its own annihilation.

Are you convinced yet of this original addiction? It is the king of all addictions. All other addictions, being secondary, would have to come from original addiction. What I am implying here is no one can even fall into any other addiction without first being addicted to the small, fear-based, egocentric self. Wow, think about it: all along we've been trying to fill our big selves, our true selves, with our small selves! "*Oy vey*," says the Jewish daughter (that's me). "Stop the train, I want to get off." Are any of you thinking that? Good, good, good. It's time to get off to get on.

So I am a recovering gambling addict, but I am also a recovering ego, small-self addict, as we all are. Even if you have not fallen into other addictions, it is so important to understand addiction from the standpoint of original addiction. I could not have remained out of my secondary addiction of gambling until I began to deal with my original, fear-based, ego-addicted thoughts. Those self-justifying thoughts are the cement of addiction and the key driving force behind relapse.

This notion of original addiction holds a huge implication for healing any addiction completely and on the deepest possible level: at its point of origin! This is the sole reason why people relapse in all other secondary addictions! It is the reason I relapsed the many times I did. The degree of risk for relapse correlates to the degree of the deeper original small-self addiction.

This is why so many of us recovering from secondary addiction become spiritually connected. It becomes even more dire to recover from original addiction because our secondary addiction can be devastating to our lives and even life threatening. In this sense, secondary addiction is a gift toward deeper soul awakening for those of us who have chosen to walk this sacred path. Recovering from my gambling addiction brought me deeper into a true spiritual connection to myself.

Traditional secondary addicts, in successful recovery, can actually lead the pack in helping everyone else toward their recovery from original addiction. As I paved the road in my own recovery, I learned that it is a road everyone needs to travel. I learned that to truly heal beyond superficial abstinence, it became imperative to go deeper into my distorted thought patterns and the way I oriented myself in the world. As I recovered from gambling, I began to recover from original addiction as well. In traditional recovery, these distorted thought patterns are known as "stinking thinking." Let's all recover from our "stinking thinking."

Secondary addicts, as they heal on the deepest level, become the role models that the rest of the world has needed. They have been so ostracized and yet, as the underdog, they can aid the recovery of everyone else! This is true because our common goal is to recover from original addiction. I've come to understand this tendency to ostracize as a fear of one's own self. When we react strongly to someone else, we are usually reacting to something unresolved within ourselves.

Have you heard of "cutting the Gordian knot"? The Gordian knot was a knot that could not be cut. It comes from the legend of Phrygian Gordium, who was associated with Alexander the Great. It is used as a metaphor for solving an intractable problem with a bold stroke.[11] Healing original addiction is the bold stroke that cuts the Gordian knot of relapse for all other expressions of addiction. With or without secondary addiction, healing original addiction is also the bold stroke for all of us to resolve our relapses into our fear-based, ego-addicted selves. This leads to ultimate healing and the return to Clarity in all of us.

Realize that the more addiction expresses itself, the more it invades the spirit and attempts to take over. In a way, it is just like Clarity becoming confused by the oil spills, to the point that eventually she has clouded her true identity and pure crystalline essence. This is true of all addiction, both secondary and original. Addiction serves as an "oil" that clouds our true identity. Any force expressing itself from the small self is, by definition, addiction-driven. Indeed, our entire lifetimes are about healing the false addictions of the ego self and returning to our true, God-connected, divine selves.

So then, how can you heal yourself from the position of the clouded self that is addicted anyway? It's quite a riddle, huh! Is it starting to resemble a dog chasing its own tail? Many recovering addicts know that the pain of separation has to become strong enough that one day we begin to wake up and see a little dot, a pinpoint, of light in the vast darkness that addiction brings. In the traditional addiction recovery world, this is referred to as "becoming sick and tired of becoming sick and tired." Original addiction also makes us "sick and tired." Let's recover and become vibrant and well.

For me, in my secondary addiction, I was consciously aware that I was hooked into gambling for so long and I still could not break out of it. I saw the point of light, but I became overwhelmed with how to get there. It seemed so very far away. I felt too meek; after all, I was in original, small-self addiction as well. I thought I had created too much of a mess in my life to ever clean it up. I was lost in self-judgment and self-condemnation (enough to fill a whole nation), and the more I self-judged, the more I stayed in addiction.

This is because addiction feeds on negativity. Negativity is like a candida for addiction. (Remember as you read on that this is about all of us, because of original addiction.) The candida of negativity, whether inwardly or outwardly directed, feeds the addict and the addict thrives on it. And it grows and grows and grows. Isn't it strange that addiction wants more and more of itself and love wants more and more of itself? Free will comes with a price if we don't choose love.

I remember one time in my early twenties, many years before my fall into gambling addiction, where I must have sensed the magnitude of what was ahead—how much there was to personally resolve in my life—and I wanted a shortcut. Deep inside, I think I knew there was work to be done that at times would be grueling. I just wanted to hurry up and get it done with so I could enjoy life, play, and simply have a good time. I loved life; I just didn't want to deal with my small self and its ego demons.

So I heard about "firewalking," led by instructors who were taught by its founder in the United States, Tolly Burkan. Since I was in my twenties I wanted self-actualization as if it was a thing that you could acquire in a moment—probably true on some level, but I just went about it the wrong way. Combined with that, I had already established a thrill-seeker energy that was trying to fill externally what felt cut off in me. I eagerly signed up for a nearby seminar and spent half of a day getting "fired up" (pardon the pun).

To prepare us, the instructor had us visualize positive memories of success and the emotional energies that went with them. We also established a positive mantra to block fear and increase our physical energy. Then off we went—fifty of us—to walk across twenty feet of red hot coals with flames licking around the edges! I brought my boyfriend, Dave, and volunteered him to walk before me—thank you, Dave! He had a beautiful protective energy about him. So we set off into the firewalk, mantra intact, and intently vibrating between our lips, "Cool moss, cool moss, cool moss..." all the way through twenty feet of fire-licking coals. Wow, it was surreal. Did I just do that? I went back and walked again.

We debriefed after the firewalking. Most everyone was fine; only one person sustained a very mild burn. I had what the instructor called "hot feet," which makes you think you've burned, because those puppies were hot, but you really haven't. I was happy, though—very happy, elated, maybe even a little boastful afterward (that should have been a warning sign), but a small price to pay for self-actualization, right? Nope. Small price, yes, but did I get the instant self-actualization I expected? This was another warning sign. Yes, step right up and you, too, can be self-actualized for the mere price of one firewalking seminar—not! They did not advertise this way; it was my young mind's interpretation.

I went back into my life with the same ego-addicted patterns as ever. What was missing? Are you guessing it? You cannot heal with the head alone; you must, must, must bring in the heart for true healing and soul resolution to occur. I did not learn that until many years later, because I spent many years trying to heal it all with my head.

This is what so many of us do. We try to resolve our emotions by justifying and cementing them as a false security, thereby becoming emotionally attached and addicted. Alternatively, we explain them away and disassociate ourselves, thereby becoming disconnected and at risk for external addictions. In either state, we have been severed from the true, love-based self and entered into the false, fear-based self. Of course, in this ego-based, small self, we don't even know we are doing this. The small self must first move through denial. This is especially challenging with original addiction as I stated earlier because, since we all have an aspect of it, who will be the one to point it out for any of us to heal it?

Addiction comes from our fear-based, false ego condition and is therefore disconnected from the true self. In this addicted energy state of fear-based and love-devoid emotions, we experience:

- anger
- hate
- pride
- greed
- blame
- bitterness
- judgment
- misery
- self-justification
- hopelessness
- unhappiness
- insecurity
- lack of faith
- lack of self-love
- self-destruction
- jealousy
- competitiveness
- control
- frustration
- selfishness
- guilt
- shame

In our love-based energy states, devoid of fear, we experience:

- joy
- faith
- trust
- inner strength
- confidence
- happiness
- caring
- sharing
- forgiveness
- openness
- passion
- freedom
- harmony
- honesty
- beauty
- compassion
- self-love
- self-appreciation
- respect
- acceptance
- peace
- balance between giving and receiving
- understanding
- positivity

These states are born of our true essence, our boundless God-connected selves.

When you read the different words, can you feel the difference in their energy? The negative, fear-based words create a "pulling" and a depleting feeling. The positive, love-based words bring a more present-centered, clear, allowing, and receptive feeling. With which words are you able to relax and breathe more easily?

Are you starting to get the bigger picture about addiction? We are all addicted and most of us are in at least partial denial. We must recognize this to begin the process of recovery, the journey back to the heart and where the true, God-based self thrives. This does not happen by justifying our emotions and becoming indignant, or by projecting any other negative energy outwardly into the world. Nothing is "justified" outside of the ego. "Justify" is an ego-based word. Can you feel the "pull" of the word?

Addiction is our ultimate distraction. Unconditional love is our birthright by which we arrived here and to which we shall return either before or after our physical death. We choose when we are ready for the divinity of this God-given love of the true self. Which one will you ultimately choose? Are you ready to find your way home?

For a long time I was not ready. Many times, though, I held

my true self stronger and tried again. Many times I fell again, feeling overwhelmed and run over by the small self playing big. To remain in this stronger state, yes, yes, I had to keep going back. Remember the emotional "muscle" building. Love, love, love, love, and with every repetition, heal!

The small self is really just like an "elf," a little mischievous creature. Here's an interesting play on the word "elf:" ELF is an acronym that stands for "extremely low frequency." It is used to describe electromagnetic signals of very low frequencies of around 60Hz.[12]   Remember, the electromagnetic frequency of the heart is 528Hz and is the frequency for transformation and miracles. I knew which frequency I really wanted to give out and receive.

So, at one point, I participated in energy healing sessions with a very gifted healer who did sound healing on me using tuning forks. This may seem strange at first, but remember our chakras vibrate to different tonal frequencies, so exposure to tuning forks by a trained practitioner is a modality for balancing our chakra energies.

In one of the sessions, relaxed and in a meditative state, I felt a tremendous welling of compassion for myself and everyone else at the casino I was frequenting. Most of the gamblers there, I came to learn, were not recreational—addicts support much of the industry. In this compassion, I saw in my mind's eye a huge, thick, cushiony, quilt-like blanket descend onto the casino and cover the entire casino, as if it had come from the heavens above.

I felt a deep, loving compassion for my fellow addicts and myself. I felt a deep love for myself and everyone there. I grieved in love for our emotional pains that had brought us to such separation. I wanted with all my heart and soul for all of us to heal. It was a deepening of love and compassion. In that moment, I was not in touch with negative self-judgments and self-condemnation at all. You cannot be in love and feel these negative energies at the same exact time. It is virtually impossible.

The enlightened path is where we return to grounding love in the heart and speaking from this place in our lives and into our relationships. Every ripple we send out is either from our true self and is therefore heart-based, or from our ego-addicted small self. Do you want to enjoy the resolution in this lifetime to enrich the divine gift of this earthly experience? This is the incredible opportunity given to us, the choice to live as heaven on earth! All of us choose, be it consciously or unconsciously. This is utterly inescapable! Choose wisely and choose consciously.

Chapter Nine

Releasing Codependence and Stepping Into Loving Self-Empowerment

So we resolve our emotions by letting go. Letting go of what, you ask? The way we think we need the world to be, our friends, our spouses, our significant others, everyone to whom we want to write the script to read as if we were their God. It is easy to dismiss ourselves from this, but think about it. We may not really mean to do this, but we can be awfully manipulating and self-deceptive. Add to this the fact that we do most of this unconsciously. Anytime we have a judgment or an expectation of another person, we are playing God in their life rather than honoring the God within them.

What would happen if instead we connected with that God part of them? We would have to remove any judgments to even begin to connect with their God-like self. What would happen if we did that? Hard stuff, huh? Feeling a bit justified? It is hard work to let go. It is very hard to do this when we've been "wronged," right? But, if you can imagine this, even partly, then you will begin to feel yourself and the world transform with that experience of letting go alone.

Our well-being is not dependent upon the responses of others, no matter how badly we've been "done wrong." We are then not being in our own power and walking within our own heart-centered selves; we are instead walking beside ourselves as victims. When we try to play God for others, we've really made *them* God by making our well-being dependent on them. So we play God by thinking we know what is good for everyone else, but then make them God for us by making our well-being dependent on them and whether they change.

We've duped our own selves. What we project reflects back to us entirely. All of this boils down to a fancy definition of codependence. Codependence is something widely talked about in the addiction recovery world and is suggestive of these words: "I need you to change in this way, as defined by me, so that I can feel fine." So, as much as we are all addicted, we are also codependent. Codependence is the fuel behind original addiction.

What then do we do when someone does us wrong in some way? We need to draw a boundary, of course. This is not done reactively or by yelling if you are grounded in the heart. This is from a statement that begins, "It's not okay with me that you...." Even if you have to shut down the communication at that time because the person continues to act out, this is still not done in a reactive tone if you are grounded in the heart. Sometimes it may require leaving that person if their abuse is in a toxic range that is too harmful for you to be in their presence. Even then, when you are ready, you can offer them compassion and wish them healing from a distance. That does not require you to be in an active relation to them—otherwise it is likely that you are addicted to making them "get it," no matter how lovingly you approach it.

Not getting this concept and staying negatively attached is a direct way to lead yourself into depression. I learned this from bouts of depression in my early adulthood. I worked so hard to fix everyone around me that I instead ended up a lonely fake yogi on a quiet solitary hill. Even though I approached them in a loving way, they weren't thrilled by my efforts to psychologically disrobe them. Needless to say, they went the other way. Much depression comes from our sense of peace and contentment being attached to the outcome of others.

You must derive your sense of well-being from within, not externally in an addicted way. Remember the negative energy of addiction-based emotions: forcing, manipulating, guilting, overpowering or any other way that you demand agreement or are offended by another's ignorance as defined by you. That is the small self's addicted ego at its un-finest! You define *you*. No one else defines you, and you don't define them. Let go and let your own self-knowing define your experience.

Be aware of your own self-manipulation and self-deception, for that is how the ego-addicted self keeps itself alive. Slick little bugger, huh? Do not let your loving approach make you think you are not coming from addiction. If you have a burning need for them to "get it," chances are you are addicted. Addiction, especially ego-based thought addiction, is sneaky and conniving. We don't want to see this because it is really hard work to be self-accountable in the truest and most complete sense. We want everyone else to get it right for our world to be fine.

We want that because it comes from a place of disempowerment where we are in our small selves and have not become grounded in the heart and in our own true self-worth and empowerment. And this is because our small scared selves, trying to control the world around us, and not thriving in the heart center, are so very afraid of annihilation. We are so afraid of more crude oil from others that we stay on the defense, not realizing that the only true healing comes from cleaning our own spills and nurturing them out of their false essence.

There's that cute little dog chasing its tail again—ruff, ruff! It's so rough! But we love those cute little puppy dogs, so let's bring the compassion into ourselves. With higher love, you still may communicate how you feel, but your well-being is not tied to the actions and responses of others. This is how you draw a boundary without being defined by others in your life.

There is something you can do besides drawing a boundary when someone is treating you wrongly. I call it exposing them to themselves. For instance, let's say that someone in your life, for example your grown child or a spouse, starts yelling at you angrily. Using the strategy of exposing them to themselves, your response would be to then state their behavior. "I see that you are distressed right now. Did you have a bad day? What is it that you need?" The idea is that when you name that person's behavior, they unconsciously become too embarrassed to continue emotionally acting out that way. Typically, they would at least quiet down. I used to confront people in such moments head on, and learned that I only got my head cut off. When someone else is directing anger your way, they have an emotional "guillotine." Save your head by staying level-headed.

If you become hurt by their behavior, you would be in an addicted state if you needed their understanding, believe it or not. I know this is difficult, but this does not mean you don't want their understanding; this means that in the big picture your well-being is not dependent on their understanding. Your well-being will remain intact when your self-preservation depends on your own self-definition.

This is very difficult in our primary relationships with our spouses, significant others, children, and parents. Of course we want to work out our relationships, but ultimately we are not always able to do so. If our well-being and self-definition comes from within, then we will be emotionally intact for the duration that the lack of understanding survives—be it an hour, a day, a week, a month, or a year.

So here's something more that can help you stay grounded in the face of someone else's unbalanced behavior. It is a reminder of the metaphor in chapter one that should be repeated: When someone is acting in a negative way toward you, they are not trying to offend you. They are only trying to act like themselves, because they have the lead role in their own drama and they are playing and perfecting their part.

This does not mean that you should not feel hurt or have other feelings related to how they are behaving. When we hurt in the heart, we are hurting from the severing of the true unconditional connection that we seek. This is different than taking it personally and then acting out ourselves. So, depersonalize the other person's bad behavior and realize that it is not about you. That will allow you to be grounded in the heart and not lost in your small ego self when you are responding to them. Some of you may have chuckled when you read that they are just trying to act like themselves. Did you feel the relief that came with the chuckle? Congratulations on removing their drama from your *response-ability*! You have had a chuckle of relief as you released their burden from you.

Now here's another tool for your self-empowerment box. This one I really enjoy. When someone is behaving in a negative way in your life, pull the positive out of the negative. Let's look at this. This is about intention and reception. As a reminder, there is a world of difference at times between the two. When you don't like someone's behavior, almost always their intention is good, even though your reception of their behavior may not be to your liking. Here is an example: a critical mother of a grown daughter with a baby of her own, keeps saying, "You are not doing it right; here's how you burp the baby," or "You're having him cry too long," or "No, leave him longer." Maybe this has gone on for a year or even several years. Finally, the daughter is burned out and wants to wring her mother's neck!

But wait, hold that wringing! What about the drama, you know the one where they have the lead role in which they are playing their part? So instead, pull the positive from the negative. Compliment their intention and depersonalize yourself from their chosen behavior toward you. Here is the same scenario using the tools I have presented here: "Mom, you know it really means a lot to me how much you care about my baby. I feel your love come through when you try so hard to help me get it right from all of your experience, and I am grateful to have such a caring mother. The baby and I are very lucky to have you." In this example, it is important that the daughter validate the mother's feelings to help her feel understood in her intention.

Then, and only then, without rushing, can the daughter move toward her own feelings on the matter and say for example, "You know, in my being a new mom, part of the excitement is discovering my own self—as a mother. It would mean so much to me if you would give me some room to find my own way through a lot more. I know you will always be there for me. And, if I have a question, I want you to know that I will always ask you. I would even welcome your suggestions as long as you will also respect my room to make my own choices."

Can you see how the daughter is grounded in the heart? Can you imagine the changed response the daughter is likely to receive? I guarantee at least silence, which is the middle response, the one that says the mother's negative energy flow has at least been interrupted. On rare occasions, with particularly insecure individuals, it may take two or three rounds.

So when you don't like another's behavior, pull the positive out of the negative and acknowledge their good intention. If you remain consistent and do not allow yourself to be emotionally pulled off balance, you would have at least softened the heart of the other person, even if only a little. And I guarantee that you would have softened your own heart tremendously.

You don't have to wait for a year or more of build-up to do it; that only makes it harder to come down from the small, hurt self that thought it was about you! In the above example, the mother may have been going through fears of not being needed, or feelings of inadequacy that she was a bad mother, now masking it as an overconfident grandmother. Whatever the case, can you see that it was about her, her stuff? It was not about the daughter or the baby at all.

We all want acknowledgment and understanding. When we get that, we no longer feel isolated in the world. We feel heard and loved — we feel relieved. And when we offer it, what a beautiful thing it is to soften the heart of a person in your life behaving in an overbearing and unconsciously scared way. You can heal others by loving them by not taking their acting out as an assault on you. To this end, you ultimately heal yourself as well.

Take a moment now and think of an example in your own life that fits this scenario of being angry and annoyed at someone else's behavior. Think about how you could change your response and have a transforming effect on both of you by pulling the positive from the negative. This is how we heal ourselves and the world!

Though all of these tools, we heal codependence as we learn to say and live by this self-directed line: "I need me to change in this way, as defined by my heart grounded in love, so that my world can feel fine."

Chapter Ten

Acknowledgment is Second to Love

Let's go a bit further in explaining the essential importance of acknowledgment, both self-acknowledgment and ac-knowledgment of others. Let's look at acknowledgment and how much we truly give and receive from this beautiful and sacred gift. Acknowledgment is second to love itself. Why is that? Think about it. We all want understanding. When we feel that we are understood, we feel acknowledged. When we feel acknowledged, we no longer feel alone and isolated in the world. Now when we are in conflict with each other, we are usually defensive about acknowledging the other.

We can also look at this on a personal level of self-acknowl-edgment. When we are in inner conflict, we are usually lack-ing self-acknowledgment. I don't mean acknowledging, "Yeah, I'm pissed." I mean acknowledging the true feeling that really has you out of sorts to begin with. This is usually about our most basic needs, for example, the need to be loved and feeling threatened by feeling unloved, or the need to be counted and feeling discounted and sad from that. With self-acknowledg-ment, we reach the authentic feelings beneath the ego's defen-sive masked feelings of anger, indignation, and hurt. You can always identify a masked feeling because you will experience emotional defensiveness around it and its ensuing pull of expectation.

Self-acknowledgment requires making yourself count enough to connect with and value your authentic feelings and needs. As a therapist, I have learned that self-acknowledgment is the first essential seed for healing any inner angst. We cannot heal until we are willing to meet ourselves in our authentic feelings and become acquainted with our heart. Without self-acknowledgment, we risk depression because we are not in a state of self-valuing.

Think of a situation in your life where you are feeling an inner conflict and see what it feels like to truly identify and acknowledge your authentic feelings, not your ego-defended hurt feelings. At first, you might find that you don't even know what the authentic feeling is because you have had it confused with your masked feeling for so long.

If you find yourself starting with "I think," change it to "I feel." A lot of us confuse our thoughts with our feelings. Or you can also respond to "I think" by then asking, "How does that make me feel?" If you then get a response to yourself of "angry" or "sad," remember that is still not the feeling as much as the mask to the feeling. You are closer, though. Then ask, "Why does this make me feel sad or angry?" or whatever masked, defensive feeling is arising. You can also do the "why game," where you continue asking yourself why you feel the way you do with each response you give yourself. With each "why" you will go deeper into your true underlying feeling. You will know when you have reached your authentic feeling because you will feel an emotional shift and an "aha" feeling when you get there. The defense will be gone and will be replaced with a feeling of deeper connection to your true self.

When you get to the feeling, really spend time with it. You might even want to expand the space for your feelings by journaling. Then when you really feel you've gotten to your authentic emotions as well as to the essential needs they represent for you, tell me how you feel. Well all right, you cannot literally tell me how you feel! Just pretend you are in a conversation with me and tell me how it feels to truly be connected to your authentic self. Do you feel your heartbeat? Do you notice the calm, the quiet? You are no longer in a reactive state. Notice that you are more in the present moment than what you are used to. You may feel a welling of emotions. Let them out, let them breathe. I am handing you a virtual tissue. You matter! Breathe consciously and stay with your authentic feelings. Breathe, feel, and relax. What a gift! Do you see?

Just a short time with self-acknowledgment leads you right to your heart and your essential true self. Inner conflict and inner turmoil are then calmed and comforted, and begin to resolve. It is this reconnection to the heart center that heals us. What have you learned about yourself as you have truly connected with your authentic self?

I invite you now to sit down somewhere comfortably, close your eyes, and feel yourself breathing some more. Consciously take in slower breaths and as you inhale and exhale, imagine your breaths coming into and out of your heart. As you do this, invite yourself to think about the people in your life that you love. Keep breathing in and then out through your heart. Imagine the many things you love about them. Breathe in and out through your heart. Imagine all of the ways they show their love to you. Breathe in and out through your heart and feel your heart and your love expand.

The most powerful key to healing any relationship is with acknowledgment of the other, whether this is with our significant others, our children, parents, friends, or bosses. It is the single most frequent therapeutic suggestion I have made to countless clients over the years to heal these hurt relationships.

What happens to acknowledgment of the other person when there is conflict in our relationships, or when we are not grounded in the heart? In a state of emotional conflict with each other, we play the "passing the ball" game as we toss back and forth to each other feelings that reflect,

"You don't understand me."

"No, you don't understand me."

"Yes, I do."

"Yes, I do," is said very quickly with no acknowledgment. Needless to say, it is not very convincing to the other person.

We feed each other "lip service" as we defend our own emotional camps. "But you don't understand me!"

Finally, with some luck, one person gives in and tries to listen to the other person. It is still very hard to be patient, but this one person slows down at least a bit. Now with one of the two people at least somewhat understood (hiccup), that first person now tries to get understanding and acknowledgment back. Chances are, while they've connected some, since they are still mostly attached to being understood, it is likely that they have rushed and done some glossing over. But a rush job is better than no job, right? By the end, there may have been understanding but it was exhausting! Still, whatever measure of release occurred from this emotional tug-of-war came from acknowledgment. The degree of acknowledgment we offer the other is directly proportional to the degree of resolution achieved. You can get there fast or slow, with lots of tugging or releasing. But, in the end, acknowledgment is the only energy that resolves the communication gap, restores love, and resolves our relationships.

Why is this so exhausting? The exhaustion is a reflection of each person getting lost in their individual human encampments and then protecting their individual tents. We are all fearful that if we acknowledge the other person first, somehow the other person won't offer the same back to us. None of us want to feel alone and missed.

What would happen if we all just took a breath and were willing to love enough, care enough, and trust enough in love to simply acknowledge the other person first? Can you feel the shift this creates? Can you feel their heart softening as you let go of your own need and offer such understanding of them from your own heartfelt space? What do you think would happen next? Our fears would have told us that if we do the acknowledging first, the other person will not do the same. But now that you can feel what this does for the other person, you can understand that it actually softens them. Then, guess what? They want and do the same thing for you.

When we love first, love follows. When we defend and shut out first, love is less likely to follow. Oh, magic of magic, wonder of wonders, how we truly lift each other up and heal each other when we step out of the fear-based, small self and walk into our own hearts. And when we do that, we are then willing to walk into the heart of another! I know of a beautiful song reflecting this by Alice Di Micele, "We Shall Lift Each Other Up" (Circle of Women, Various Artists, 1997) The song begins with:

> Humble yourself in the sight of your sister. You got to bend down low and, humble yourself in the sight of your brother. Ask him what he knows and we shall lift each other up, higher and higher...

So you see, we find the heart of the other buried within our own hearts! Are you getting the sacred importance of acknowledgment? Feel how important this is! It is an adjunct, perhaps the most important adjunct to, love.

Let's take this even deeper and make it more personal for you. Recall and then imagine a situation in your own life when you had a conflict with someone and this fear-based ego-infused dynamic played out. In this example, choose anyone close: a friend, lover, or spouse. Imagine the scene where the conflict occurred. What were you feeling at the time? What were you wearing? What was he or she wearing? Make it real in your memory. Where were you when the scene played out? Was anyone else there? What was being said in the original scenario? Recreate the original scene.

Then when you have it, change the scene to one where you step out of your own attachments and acknowledge the feelings of the person or people in the scene first. Breathe with this imagined changed experience. Be with it. What are you saying differently now? How do your words change as you shift to your softened, heart-based self and release your clenching, fear-based self? What do you notice in the other person now that you did the acknowledging first? What do you notice in yourself? Is there a sense of calm and of being present in the here and now?

Do you feel the connection in your heart open and also receive the heart connection of the other person? Wow! Change begins with you! Look at how you are now joined. No one feels isolated on an island or alone anymore. Acknowledgment moves mountains.

In families, too, imagine this playing out as parents to our children. We want so very badly for them to learn the life lessons we know they need, that we are not often willing to really acknowledge their feelings first. Now that does not mean acknowledge them to disagree with them, it means really stepping into their world and trying to understand what they must be feeling. If you are not sure, ask them. They will probably want to tell you because of how it makes them feel to be asked. Now, if you've been defining them for long time and not listening to them, then they may not trust you at first. But, if you really help them feel your sincerity, they will probably come around and tell you how they feel. Even if they are way off-base and totally distorted, stay with them in their feelings, and do not become judgmental or reactive. It's not about you, anyway; it's about them. The more you ask them how they feel, the more you will help them get to their authentic feeling—that feeling is never distorted.

Now you've learned something precious about your child. Please don't get concerned that you are giving away your authority as a parent. That is not the case at all. When you acknowledge them first, they are more likely to respond; in fact, they are much more likely to respond to your guidance. You have validated them first and helped them to feel that they matter. They will more naturally want to hear what you have to say because you will have connected with them on a heart level, not on a level of the ego tug-of-war.

If you are not a parent, there may be children in your life you could do this with. In fact, you may be the first one to acknowledge them where no one else has before if they are in an emotionally unbalanced home environment. They may not have received such validation from their parents. When you offer this in your relationship to them, for instance as a teacher, scout leader, aunt or uncle, it is a sacred gift to them.

To complete our understanding of acknowledgment, we must consider a deeper aspect that is essential in our path toward wholeness. This is the acknowledgment of the child self that I mentioned in the prelude, the child we grew up around. Our child self invariably experienced hurts, in some cases even on a traumatic level. The memories and accompanying feelings are still there, stored in our cells.

So acknowledgment, to this end, means that we can have a dialogue with that hurt inner child self. I must express a note of loving caution, however. If you've been through significant trauma in your childhood and have not worked with a guide or therapist to help you through this, then it might be a beautiful and loving gift to yourself to do so. This can be a very overwhelming process to go through alone if you've never moved through these emotions before. In fact, I advise you to skip this section on your own if you are aware of any childhood trauma or abuse you had suffered. I recommend enlisting the help of a qualified therapist to support you in healing these hurt parts of yourself. That guide or therapist can be a voice of acknowledgment while helping you move toward self-acknowledgment and love for your inner child. Use your discernment as you read on.

You can invite your child self to communicate with you and tell you how he or she is feeling. You inner child may need to express repressed and painful emotional experiences that need to be healed more in-depth. One approach to this is through automatic writing with the right and left hands. Let your non-dominant hand represent your inner child. Ask him or her about feelings that never got acknowledged.

You can even ask your inner child about hopes and dreams that got lost along the way. You might recall in the prelude that my inner child was deeply connected with writing and helped me reconnect to that part of me. What your inner child has to tell you can also be precious in rediscovering forgotten and creative parts of you. When awakened, it can bring great meaning to your present life.

Here is a guided meditation to connect with your inner child in a gentle and loving way. To do this meditation, please refer to the box that follows entitled, "Connecting with your Child Self." I will use the feminine voice, so if you are male, please imagine the masculine voice in this meditation. For your ease of meditating, please go to my website for an audio download of this meditation, available separately in both genders, at *www. ultimate-healing.com.*

CONNECTING WITH YOUR CHILD SELF

Get comfortable and start consciously breathing in slowly and exhaling slowly and deeply. Relax and breathe in this more conscious way for a few moments as you begin to visualize. You are walking down a street in the neighborhood you grew up in, at your present age, taking a stroll today. Notice your surroundings. What do you see around you? Are there any trees? Are you in the city on the concrete or are you in the country? What do you hear? Notice if the scene makes you feel anything as you take in your surroundings. Breathe... As you take this stroll, know that you are going to a special place today. You are taking a walk to a place where you used to play outside as a child. It may be school grounds, a friend's backyard, a park: go to wherever that place is and continue connecting with what is around you.

When you arrive, you see your child self and your child self sees you. Your eyes meet and you begin walking toward each other. Notice how old your child self is. As you notice her, does your child self seem happy, sad? Can you connect with her feelings? If there was any noise in the background, that has disappeared. There is a quiet calm in the air as you approach each other. When your child self reaches you, tell her that you are so happy to see her today. Your child self may greet you with a hug, she may cry, seem angry, or seem happy. Whatever it is, tell your child self that you honor her feelings and would like to know what she is feeling today.

There is a beautiful willow tree up ahead and you ask your child self to sit down with you there. You reach out to her and she takes your hand. Together, you walk over to the tree. You sit down with your child self by the tree and invite her to share anything she would like with you today. Listen to whatever your child self has to tell you and acknowledge her feelings fully. Ask your child self if she has more to share. When she has finished, acknowledge her in love and gratitude. Ask your child self if it's okay to give her a hug. If it is not, honor her wishes and tell her that you love her. If it is okay, then give your child self a hug. Thank your child self for spending time with you today.

Acknowledge, acknowledge, and have tissues, especially if you never allowed yourself to go as deeply into the feelings of your inner child self as this before. This is very essential work in grounding yourself much more deeply into your heart on your life journey. There is no more precious gift to give your inner child than the voice he or she was never able to have, never invited to have, or perhaps never even knew how to express.

So, again, acknowledgment is the most direct adjunct to connecting in love both within ourselves—deep within ourselves—and with the people in our lives. Can you see how the same divine beauty of acknowledgment can play out between friends, siblings, groups (like in the workplace), and, yes, even countries, in resolving our differences? Would there really be a place for war anymore?

Chapter Eleven

The Wounded Healer and Trusting
Your Discernment

Many of us enlist helpers in our personal journey along the way, professionals who we choose for support to help us move through our emotional challenges and growing pains. These would be therapists, doctors, alternative health practitioners, or clergy. I strongly encourage you, if you haven't already, to seek such a guide. This is a loving and beautiful choice for you to make. It is important to choose and honor what approach feels most comfortable to you. Many roads can effectively guide you back to your true divine self and living grounded in the heart.

Remember, when you turn to any one of these individuals for help, that they are human, too. Use discernment in your choosing. Never assume that the person you have hired has worked through all of their stuff. Believe me, because we are human, this is probably not the case. In fact, if you meet someone who seems to exude that they are 100 percent self-actualized and resolved—and they are actually broadcasting this—I suggest you go the other way quickly and do not waste your time and money.

I share this with you because I truly care about you and I honor your sacred journey, which should always be handled with the utmost respect and care. I also know the tremendous value of guides and therapists along the way to help you in your journey, not just because I am a therapist, but because of the guides who have helped me in my own life. From my own experience, I have learned how hurtful and potentially damaging a severely out of balance guide or therapist can be, as well as the tremendous difference in a guide who is grounded and holds the sacred space.

I firmly uphold as a therapist, that the most essential quality all people in the helping/healing modalities must have is the ability and commitment to "hold the ground" and "hold the space." They must understand this necessity and sacred responsibility. What am I talking about here? What does it mean for guides or therapists to do this? It means that they must be grounded within themselves enough that they can serve as the anchor point for your journey of self-discovery. It means that under no circumstances should they ever be in a reactive state toward you.

There is only one potential exception and that is if you were to become personally threatening to them or abusive in any way. However, unless there is physical risk, there is still no reason for them to lose their ground. Perhaps they may need to set a limit, at the most, but not to be in a reactive state with you and lose their ground. Though you have invested time, money, and personal involvement, I would seriously suggest moving on unless and only unless that guide is able to become aware and take accountability.

Realize that if your practitioner reacts to you, that is a form of abuse. You are the one working through your emotional challenges at that time. Your emotional triggers should surface because you are there to work through your personal challenges. Your guide, then, has the high responsibility to manage his or her own emotional state so that this does not become the subject of your process.

Let me give you an example. Let's say that in my role as a therapist, I ask a question to a client or move in a direction that triggers an emotional pain the client is not ready to deal with. If the client then becomes verbally defensive to me, it is my job and utmost responsibility to stay with that client in their process. It is my sacred responsibility to remain grounded within myself and not take the client personally, thereby making it about me. This is what I mean by "holding the ground."

I recall a time I was late starting a therapy session and my client became angry. That was a perfect therapeutic opportunity to help the client and by no means an invitation for my reaction to his anger. After telling me off for making him wait, the client went outside to smoke a cigarette and calmed down. I had been only ten minutes late in wrapping up a prior session, so I could have chosen to go out of balance and become indignant and defensive over his reaction. That is what a weak therapist would do. Instead, he came back in, I acknowledged his feelings, did not make it about me, and he was able to use the session beautifully to work through some old abandonment issues.

Of course I am not advocating that you go off on your therapist (though I do have soft pillows in my office)! I am saying that the guide you choose needs to hold the ground, this sacred ground, so that you can feel safe enough emotionally to do your work and ask for what you need. You absolutely deserve that and no less. Your guide is entering into a sacred space with you, your sacred space, and you are inviting that guide to join you on your journey.

Also, as a strong therapist, if my client questions where the therapeutic process is going or needs my clarification, I can handle concerns without taking it personally. You should expect no less of any therapist or guide with whom you engage.

I am laying all of this out for you because I know what it is like to put time, emotional investment, and money into the work, and also because I understand and uphold the tremendously sacred role of therapists and other professional guides. You deserve their accountability to the process. I consider my role as a therapist to be a very sacred role, and it must be handled with the highest form of self-responsibility.

Any helpers who are not ready to do that would be doing a

disservice to their clients and invariably to themselves. You deserve this measure of self-responsibility from them. You are sacred and your work is sacred. When helpers are truly holding the space, you are able to go the furthest with the personal work of your sacred journey. You should not have to be distracted or derailed by their stuff, even subtly.

The helping professions attract a plethora of wounded healers. Wounded healers can by far be the most powerful and effective of healers because they have truly "been there," but only if they have worked through a significant amount of their personal challenges, can recognize their own triggers, and not project them into the therapeutic relationship. Ideally, as I know you will understand at this point, the most powerful healers are grounded in the heart. That said, even if they are not fully grounded in the heart, they can still be effective as long as they hold the space and hold their ground. Your work is sacred; you are sacred.

Many alternative guides, such as practitioners of energy healing modalities, do not have significant or adequate training in therapeutic practices. Some of them have taken a short weekend course to then practice their modality. Learning a technique does not alone make them adequately prepared to practice it. It is not their fault that they may be ill-prepared. Their intent may be pure but they have not been adequately trained in the therapeutic relationship. Traditional therapists are at least trained to objectively hold the sacred space and the ground, though there may even be a professional therapist not resolved enough to effectively do this.

Granted, there are also many deeply talented, highly skilled, and well-resolved practitioners, both traditional and alternative, who are psychologically and spiritually able to hold the space and the ground. Just love and respect yourself enough to be discerning and trust your own sense.

Unconsciously, there is a tendency for many people to assign a lot of power to their therapist or guide. Should your therapist or guide act out, if you are giving away your power, you might mistakenly think that the problem originated with you. It is emotionally dangerous to make anyone more powerful than you, because you are then vulnerable to their stuff. Be careful out there. Trust your own inner guidance, first and foremost, and, if something feels off to you in the energy of the relationship, pay attention. Most of the time, if it smells like doo-doo, it is doo-doo! Do not put the practitioner higher up than yourself. Love and trust yourself enough to be discerning.

There is one extra note of caution regarding guided experiences collectively known as "energy work," because this type of process can be very powerful. Energy healing modalities get below our ego and small self's defenses and help us go deeper, often more quickly, into our true authentic selves. When you go deeper, and are connecting spiritually through this type of soul work, it is all the more imperative for your guide to be grounded and hold the sacred space.

What would fill my heart with joy is just to know that you are out there taking care of yourself, using discernment, and valuing your own intuitive sense so that you do not turn your guides into idols when they are just as human as you are. I want so much for you to be in your own power, even when you are learning about stepping into your own power. In this way, you can protect your sacred work and the necessity to be with someone who truly knows how to hold their ground and hold the space.

Chapter Twelve

Soul Contracts and the Lessons We Lovingly Set Up

My spiritual work is mine. Your spiritual work is yours. None of us can dismiss ourselves from this or we are not living fully alive. Our soul lessons come in every possible form. We don't get to consciously choose. We do, however, seem to have a built-in divine pre-wiring that brings to us whatever we need for our personal and spiritual evolution. Honor that, so that no matter how painful the journey may be, you value the experience to gain the needed soul lesson. Deepen your soul work by embracing the lessons you create along the way for your ultimate resolution in this grand journey.

Do not go into victimhood and miss the lesson or your soul will lovingly set it up again. Remember, this internal auto-correct mechanism is really our soul crying out and loving us so unconditionally as to make sure we get any lesson we need in order to spiritually evolve ourselves more fully. Following Rumi's sacred words, don't go back to sleep.

The breeze at dawn has secrets to tell you.
Don't go back to sleep.

You must ask for what you really want.

Don't go back to sleep.

People are going back and forth across the doorsill

where the two worlds touch.

The door is round and open.

Don't go back to sleep.[13]

We navigate through the dramas we create in order to re-solve ourselves. I'm sure you've noticed that we love ourselves enough to create the same dramas over and over unceasing-ly until we work out our stuff of life. Remember the tree, the beautiful tree: it could not grow sideways. It self-corrected. We are in a perpetual state of self-correction. Again, this is not be-cause we are bad or that we are to be ashamed. This is because we love ourselves unconditionally enough to bring whatever lessons we need in order to go home.

I am speaking of that place of home in the heart. This is the grand journey, the journey home to the heart! We must let go of the head game to arrive fully in the heart. Some refer to this jour-ney as the "thirteen-inch" journey from the head to the heart. It is the longest journey in which you will ever participate, and the most sacred and ultimately beautiful journey in this earth walk. When we fully arrive in the heart and can come unshakably and utterly from love then we have truly arrived home.

You are growing up through life, in all likelihood living out your patterns lovingly and unconsciously acting like yourself. A beautiful golden chariot comes with you from your birth. You don't know that some time in those very early years you step in. Your higher self is in the driver's seat with a copy of your soul contract that you came here to fulfill. This higher self is consciously connected to the divine source and always knows exactly what you need. Your loving higher self guides you through life to some beautiful places and experiences and some very painful ones. Sometimes you want to curse out this driver and say, "Why are you bringing me here? This isn't any fun! I don't deserve this; what did I do to deserve this?"

Ahh, but you must trust in your higher self, because no

matter how painful the experience, your guide knows exactly where you need to go in life and what you need to experience in order to grow up straight. Your guide loves you enough to keep you from growing sideways. There is no judgment from your guide, only loving kindness. It may not seem kind at times, but your guide is there holding your hand through the most painful of experiences. Can you sense him or her? He or she is with you and has been here all along untiringly and unconditionally. Your higher self is like your earth angel. Have you ever met her? Do you know him? Try to feel your higher self now.

I will share with you the following guided meditation as a very nice way to connect with your inner guide, your higher self, and to go deeper in the soul lesson of resolving an unresolved hurt. To do this meditation, please refer to the box below entitled, "Connecting with Your Inner Guide." For your ease of meditating, please go to my website for an audio download of this meditation at *www.ultimate-healing.com*.

CONNECTING WITH YOUR INNER GUIDE

Imagine a scene where you are walking on a very peaceful path in the woods. There are birds chirping overhead. Off in the distance, you hear water flowing in a stream, gurgling over the rocks and giggling in its surrender. You feel a slight breeze softly touching your face, your shoulders, and your hair. You breathe in the air. It is fragrant. Spring is in the air with new life awakening. Flowers are blooming and you smell their clean scents celebrating the day at hand. The soil is fresh and you take in the scent of the earth. You feel your feet crunching along leftover leaves from the winter. The sound of the stream gets louder and you soon see it in your view. As you approach the stream, you see a big flat rock and decide to sit upon it and relax. You stretch as the warmth of the sun greets you.

As you are sitting down and taking in the surroundings, you see a man or woman in the distance (whoever comes to you, so trust your higher consciousness; I will use the masculine for simplicity now). He exudes a very peaceful calm state. You sense self-assurance and love emanating from him. He gently approaches you and introduces himself to you as your higher guide. He explains that he is your inner intuitive self. He invites you to go on a ride with him in his chariot. He beckons, and you see behind him what appears to be a beautiful, golden-winged chariot. He seems so loving; you become curious and tell him yes. He sits down and invites you to do the same. You take a seat beside him.

He explains he is going to take you to a scene in your adult life where someone had been hurtful to you and something had remained unresolved. He explains that you are safe now and that no harm can come to you.

The chariot takes off, and you fly through the air gently and comfortably to this place with your guide. Soon you arrive. He tells you to notice and observe what is happening in the scene. Who is there? What is being said? Where are you? How far back are you in your adult life? Notice what the surroundings feel like to you. What do they look like? Listen to what is being said and notice what you are feeling. When you have that, he tells you to let him know. Take some time now in the scene and, when you are ready, let him know.

He then takes you back to the woods and the stream where he guides you to breathe deeply in through the nose and release very deeply into the abdomen and then breathe deeply all the way up from the abdomen and then release like letting all of the air out of a balloon. He tells you to repeat this five times filling and releasing the air as if from a balloon. Take some time now to do this. When you have completed it, let him know. He asks you how you are feeling. Notice this feeling.

Then he tells you that you will be traveling again in the chariot to the same scene, but this time it will be different. Off you go with him, and soon you arrive. He asks you to see the scene but with a difference. This time all of the players in the scene are connected in love through the heart. You are to connect through the heart as well. He tells you to imagine what they would be saying if they were grounded in the heart and coming from love. Even though this is not what originally happened, he still tells you to imagine this. He asks you to hear what they are saying and experience what you are feeling as they say these loving words to you. He tells you to sit with it and really hear and take into your heart what they are saying as if it is real. When you feel complete with this, let him know. He tells you that you will now be departing the scene, and off you go back down to that beautiful serene space in the woods.

He moves you through the same breathing, but this time he tells you to go past five breaths if needed, not to count, but to keep breathing in and out consciously while he talks to you. You breathe deeply in through the nose and release very deeply into the abdomen, and then breathe deeply all the way up from the abdomen, releasing as if you are letting all the air out of a balloon. Keep breathing this way as you continue to listen.

He invites you to forgive them for what they were not able to offer you. He tells you that they are moving through their own healing as well and they are unaware of what they do not know. He invites you to forgive them for how they were lost and how it may have hurt you. He asks you to love them as you realize that the first scene was not about you; they were lost and acted out of their own life dramas. Somewhere in their inner psyches, they desired to come from love but had been too fearful to do so. He also asks you to forgive yourself for what you were not able to offer them and for any way you may have acted out of your small self's fear.

He asks you to breathe healing energy into your heart and visualize your emotional hurt as black smoke exiting out of your body from wherever it needs to be released. On the outward breath, you are breathing out black smoke and watching it exit your body anywhere it is has been trapped. On the inward breath, you breathe in white, healing, soothing light. He tells you that this healing light comes straight from the heavens and that angels are breathing it into you. Again you breathe out black smoke and watch it leave your body, breathing in the white, healing, angelic light. He tells you to repeat this until you no longer see the black smoke.

You are now filled with white angelic healing light, and he tells you it is time to say goodbye for now. He tells you before he goes that he is always with you, and that all you ever need to do is call upon him. He suggests that all the answers lie within you, that ultimately you are your own true healing guide. You must only ask with the heart for the answers you need and connect with the heart to receive them. With this, he departs and you say "goodbye" knowing that he resides within you.

We have everything we need to heal ourselves. Most importantly, even when the key players in our lives get it wrong and are severed from their own hearts, we can, as long as we are grounded in our own hearts, let go of the need for them to get it right, heal ourselves with our own inner compassion, and forgive them their unconscious and unintended ignorance. They do not need to understand you for you to heal your angst. They are not about you and you are not about them. They are about them and you are about you. You need only to focus on your own soul lessons. Remember, we are coming from the lower self and addiction when we need them to change for us. Release and breathe, release and breathe. Learn your soul lessons and lovingly wish for them the same.

I recall a prayer from going to the synagogue as a child. The English version is:

Help us to return to you, oh Lord, for then shall we truly return, renew our days as in the past.

The Hebrew version is:

Hashivenu Adonai elecha vena-shuvah, kadesh, kadesh yamenu, kadesh yamen kekedem.

This prayer comes from Judaism, my religion of origin, and is a prayer of returning to our divine source. Connect with the higher part of you that arrived with you in this lifetime. Step into the golden chariot and allow your higher self to guide your lessons of the soul.

Chapter Thirteen

To the Refinery We Go

Earlier you met Clarity. Remember that you are Clarity: beautiful, unstained, pure, clear, receptive, trusting, open, vibrant, and full of love. Your essence is like crystal clear, vibrant water with a full spectrum of colors in your sacred reflection.

So why is it so hard to return to this sacred space of our true being? We began to answer the question as we learned about oil spills and the resulting original addiction of the small fear-based self. Clarity became confused by the oil spills to the point that eventually she clouded her true identity and pure, crystalline essence.

The negative effect of these oil spills on ourselves as Clarity, have brought us to oil-stained feelings of ineffectiveness and inadequacy. These pervasive and distractive feelings, when unresolved, overshadow our relationships and lead to our reactions even when we are not directly aware of this. They impede and affect our emotional energy flow and how we show up in our relationships. It is so important that we become aware of the extent to which we are not resolved in love, because so much of this lies within our psyches unconsciously. This creates our automatic responses and defenses that stunt our true soul growth.

Let's talk about "muscle testing" self-love to help you understand this impact further. The degree to which we are or are not in a loving state toward ourselves can be shown through testing the strength of our muscles. In a state of self-love, our muscles are stronger. In a state of self-deprecation, our muscles are weaker.

Overall, muscle testing is a direct way to know what input, either from ourselves or others, disrupts our balance versus what input restores our balance. It is a kinesthetic way to test the energetic effects of our thoughts, emotions, and even food or vitamins on our body's energy system. It can be used to test for allergies, proper supplementation, causal factors in diseases, treatment of imbalances, and even the effect of our beliefs and attitudes.

Remember, we are made up of energetic vibrations. Everything that we take in from the world around us, as well as what we derive from within us, is also made up of energetic vibrations. When the energetic circuits of the body are out of balance, you might say they "turn off." When we balance our body's energy, we return to a state of health and balance. This shows up in muscle testing.

There are several ways to muscle-test yourself. Here is a very simple and effective approach: Hold the index finger and thumb of one hand together, index finger against thumb, and loop this through the index figure and thumb of your other hand like a chain link. To test, you will try to pull your fingers apart when asking a question. Make contact most with the tips and less with the pads of the fingers for the best effectiveness. A "no" answer to a question will result in the fingers coming easily apart when you try to pull them. A "yes" answer will result in the fingers staying strong and not pulling apart. When you are testing, pull against your fingers just hard enough to test the spring of the muscle but not so hard that the muscle becomes fatigued. If you are not concentrating, your fingers may slide but not pull apart, causing the answer to feel unclear. When this happens, try it again and concentrate further.

To practice, in order to get the feel of muscle testing, make statements while muscle testing with obvious yes/no correlations, such as, "My name is _____" (fill in with your name, and then again with a name that is not yours) or, "The color of that wall is _____."[14]

Now, let's pre-test self-love. First, I want you to walk over to a mirror, take a few slower and deeper breaths, and look into your eyes and say aloud, "I love you _____" (fill in your name). Put the book down and really do this. It can be a tremendously powerful exercise in getting in touch with yourself and where you are in your need for personal resolution. If you harbor any sense of inadequacy in your spirit you will feel difficulty in saying this and feeling it in the heart.

Let's now muscle-test self-love. Say "I love you" with your name to yourself aloud again, this time while doing the muscle test, and notice whether you are able to hold your fingers linked together or whether they pull apart. Are you surprised? Many are.

Let's test it a little further with another powerful method of muscle testing. Find someone you have a trusting connection with and ask them to help you with this. First, hold out your dominant arm and have them press down on the forearm to test for natural resistance. Relax your arm for a moment. Next, hold your arm up again, and have them press down again while you say "I love you_____" (fill in your name) aloud. If you have any feelings of inadequacy you will not be able to hold up your arm very well when your friend pushes down.

Don't worry if you are not able to hold up your arm up very well or hold your fingers together with the first method, because most of us are not resolved in truly loving ourselves and may not even be consciously aware of this. I know, I know— there I go picking the hardest one to possibly muscle-test. I do that because I want for you the greatest possible resolution and unfolding. I want for you to know what it feels like once and for all to arrive, fully arrive in your heart, live your life through that heart space as many possible moments as you can, and stay awake to your true beautiful nature! When we consciously enter this path of awakening, we are on this path for the rest of our lives.

So why do we have to keep going back? To answer this

important question further, I will share with you a metaphor:

Every day, each and every one of us wakes up and goes to work at a refinery. I'll bet you didn't know that you have been working at a refinery, huh? You see, we go to work to remove the crude oil spills we've received so that we can restore the divine, pure, crystalline, full spectrum water that is our original essence. Clarity's oil stains were not her fault. Yet, as adults, we are responsible for our stains and healing them. So we wake up every morning and go to a refinery where we clean up the spills and their resulting stains. And we return and return yet again because we love ourselves enough to do this.

What a beautiful word, "refine." See, you are already fine; you were never not fine, so you just go back and refine yourself even more. As you refine yourself, you purify the divine waters of your birth name, and clean the oil, for your essence to shine through.

There are many who will not know they are in a refinery. To them, we can offer loving compassion and wish for them that they will work through their fears and wake up in their journey. To some, they will even act out of fear and behave in negative ways. To them, we can also offer loving compassion, wish for them a quieting and calming of their spirits, and wish them courage in waking up in their journey.

Always remember, you are not responsible for their *clarity* or lack thereof. So it is not your job to fix their oil spills nor are they likely to let you. It is only your responsibility to clean up the oil spills that have affected *you* and let your beautiful, crystalline, full spectrum of colors shine through and reflect you in your essence.

Please don't be too quick to conclude that you are not one to try to change other people in your life. Have you ever said something like, "I would be fine if you would just..." or "I'm mad at you because you did not..."? These are lines that, in effect, mean, "I need you to be this way for my world to be fine." No matter how justified you feel, these are all red flags that you are not living your life as unconditionally as you may want to believe. In fact, feelings of justification alone are by themselves giant red flags. Remember these are feelings of codependence and original addiction.

Clear your oil spills and rediscover your "Clarity." She waits for you. When you return to her, your shining light will affect others, some consciously and some unconsciously. To those who are consciously affected, they will be inspired to do the same. To them I say from my heart, "I love you and welcome you to your conscious awakening."

And to some others, they will be affected unconsciously. A number will feel an inner desire to wake up in themselves, too. To them I say from my heart, "I love you. Follow that beautiful road to your heart and do not be confused by your fears." Some will be unconsciously afraid and will act out. They will try to take you down in some way, put you down, or just leave you. They will react in fear to your light. And to them I say from my heart, "I love you, and I honor that you are just afraid and not yet ready for your return to your heart. I wish for you that, when you are ready, you may recognize your anger and attempts to control simply as fear and know that you are loved, and good enough, and not defective."

The distractions from love that are our oil stains come to us in infinite ways. These stains are the fractal teachers of our soul. Yet, the path back to the whole self is exactly the same for each and every one of us. This is the path of returning to heart-grounded love that allows us to clear the oil spills that created our stains and send our refined ripples from that place of unconditional love and acceptance.

Even those of us who have been on a conscious psycho-spiritual path for many years will go back to our refineries. We get thrown off balance because we have had a lifetime of not being fully grounded in our hearts. That is why when we get bumped around, we have to return yet again to do our work of the soul and fulfill our contracts. Our golden chariot awaits our embarking. Our faithful guide directs the journey.

So I will tell you a story of my own refining of the oils of fear and small self that happened this morning. In this story, I was challenged to resolve old oil stains of inadequacy and ineffectiveness.

I had been carrying around hundreds of pieces of paper

from years of inspiration and soul learning that I felt with great certainty in my heart, if put together, would be the book I wanted to write. For a long time, I had gathered and scattered them all over my life, just as they were cluttered all over my spirit. I did not realize at that time that my small self, in its attempt to be big, was keeping them scattered so that I would not be able to put them together to offer to people.

My true self knew I had a value to offer that could really help others, as this value had helped me over the years and many of my clients. But my small, fear-based self, as in all of our ego-addicted selves, wanted to survive and knew it would not if I stepped fully into my true divine power. So my small self came like a laughing wind and scattered my papers and their creative muse and offerings.

You see, since the ego-infused, small self fears its own annihilation, any time a higher truth comes into the conscious mind, the small self knows that it may not be needed anymore. Then it does cute little tricks to stay alive. It quietly puts on its combat boots—and, oh, you can be sure it tries to be subtle so it does not get caught. It is "Coyote Trickster." In Native American traditions, the coyote comes to teach us our life lessons but with a twist and a trick. Coyote, being the master trickster, is even fooled by his own trickery!

Well, I was at least in touch with my desire to write a book, and at one point a friend of mine suggested that I go buy a basket. "A basket," I thought. "What a wonderful way to honor all my sacred little pieces of paper." So, off I went to buy a beautiful basket. By the time I had bought this great basket, I had put more energy into the basket than my writing! Oh my, the unconscious fears of the small self played on to keep from losing itself. The poem I shared in chapter seven, "The Trickster," reflects this self-preserving aspect of fear and the small self.

Well, I did write at least a little bit at that point in time, about five pages or so. Then, a couple of years later I wrote a few more pages. I did, however, continue to write and amass more and more inspirational pieces of paper. This was a humorous tug of war between my divine, God-connected self and my fear-based, ego-addicted small self. "Hah, no biggie," spouted my small self ever so full (or *fool* we might say) of itself as it happily continued to scatter. I began to realize, though, that calculations were putting me three lifetimes down the road at least for finishing my first book!

Hmm, for a moment, my small self was not looking. It was grooming "its-elf" in the mirror and thereby missed a different reflection.   I had heard about the writer's retreat I previously mentioned. Sedona, Arizona, where it would be held, is a place very dear to my heart, so I happily signed up. My small self did not turn around in time to stop me, and off I went.

Prior to the writer's retreat, Tom, the workshop leader, had said not to bring my little pieces of paper. He said they would block my creative process. I thought to myself, "How could these precious pearls that were my heart possibly block my creative process?" So I brought them with me anyway, but promised myself I would try hard not to look at them, kind of a little private security blanket. I couldn't bring my beautiful basket that I housed them in, so instead I put them in a bag. I didn't realize until I arrived in Sedona and pulled them out of my suitcase what the writing on the outside of the bag said. I was in for a chuckle! The bag was from Carnival Cruise lines and it said, "Take me home, I'm stuffed"!

One day before the retreat commenced, I met a very interesting man at the Java Love Café in Sedona. He was a writer, and I had overheard him talking. He had mentioned to the person he was speaking with a calendar date that happened to be my birth date, so I perked up and walked over to him to inquire. He introduced himself as "Rob" and conveyed that he was soon to be giving a premier talk on his writing about the work of Carlos Castaneda.

I told him about the writer's workshop I would be attending and my pieces of paper I would soon be "smuggling in." He responded with his perspective as a writer and explained to me, if you write from what you have already written, you are writing from "secondary source" that has already happened in your life. He added that this is not effective because we are all changing every day. He concluded that if instead you write from purely the moment at hand, you are much more likely to connect with the pure creative energy that comes from your true self. I was amazed, as I shared with Rob that this was, almost to the exact wording, what Tom had said we must to do. Rob, of course, agreed that Tom was on the right track for all of us fortunate enough to have chosen him as the leader for a writer's retreat.

So, fast forward to the second day of the retreat. I was halfway through the day and had still not peeked in my "stuffed" bag of inspiration. I had promised myself not to peek except only in the case of an extreme writer's freak-out moment. Kind of like that cigarette you see encased in glass with the message that implies, "Break open only in case of extreme addiction takeover!" In this case, as with all addiction, it would have been an extreme small-self addiction take-over. After two days of not peeking, by the end of the second day, I started to feel like I was running dry and went into precious pieces of paper withdrawal!

Coyote Trickster saw his chance! Fear crept in and my small self's ego shape-shifter whispered not so sweet "nothings" in my ear disguised as "something." "What if I am not a writer after all? What if this is all the inspiration I really have to offer people? Maybe I'm done. There is nothing more to write, and all of this was just for me to find out that it's time to go home and do something I'm already good at."

Coyote was having a field day and continued to happily project his voice through me in disguise as mine. "Silly me, here I am trying to start a new creative venue when I am only half-baked in my other venue as an artist." My small self, that loyal ego soldier, sure was fighting for its little life! But I didn't know it, you see, because our little ego soldiers work very hard to convince us that this small soldier self is who we truly are.

We have an epidemic of the small self in a delusional state among us—we do not recognize our inherent greatness! So, my little soldier self continued and attempted to rob me blind while working hard to make sure I could not see. Realizing he did not really have enough of my attention yet, he threw a zinger my way knowing how much I love to have my feet on the earth exploring in nature. Throwing his voice through me,

Coyote, as soldier and shape-shifter continued: "I could always quit this god-awful writer's retreat, with this taskmaster, Tom, who won't let me look at my notes even once, and go hiking in beautiful Sedona in the red rocks I love so much."

A little light then crept in and interfered with Coyote's shade, as I considered, "But that would really be some expensive hiking, hmm...." Little ego soldier shape-shifter, trying to make me think it was the big *kahuna*, almost lost a little ground again on that one.

Do you see what was happening? My small self was ready to take over because we find it so scary to face the true divine power of who we really are. Remember, the small self fears annihilation, so it is always happy to come in and help out, per say. It will try to do so in subtle ways so it does not get caught.

So, never tiring of "its-elf," my dear, loving, small self said to me last night, "Hey I've got an idea. We will just peek at the pieces of paper and write little sentences of themes out of them just in case we get stuck, but we'll promise not to look unless we are really stuck, okay?" Now how could I resist that nice "kindhearted" offering? Do you get this, though? It sounds like addiction, doesn't it? "C'mon, one little hit won't hurt you. Just one 'line,' no one will know." My small self had me—well, almost.

Convinced this was a fair-minded plan, and with my small loyal soldier breathing a sigh of relief and wiping the sweat off of its brow, the next morning I went to breakfast with my precious pillow of "stuffed" pieces of paper about to ingest my first "line." After I ordered my breakfast, I was finally going to stick my hand in the cookie jar. Yeah! Well, just as I stuck my paw in and started to pull out my precious pearls, Valerie, one of Tom's assistants walked into the restaurant. I looked up at her sheepishly, silently gasping, as I clutched my precious pieces of paper and said, "Oh dear, you caught me red-handed."

She looked lovingly and knowingly my way, realizing what I was about to do and said, "Now, Caren, put the pieces of paper back." I hesitated. "Now, Caren, put the papers back. You don't need them."

"But," I protested, "Can I just explain why?" I feebly hoped for just one small teensy-weensy snort of precious paper.

She exclaimed lovingly, "Put the paper back in the bag, Caren!" I looked up and clasped them tighter, making my best attempt at forlorn childish eyes. This apparently was not very convincing on my forty-seven-year-old face.

Firmly but lovingly, she repeated, "Caren, put them back in the bag."

"But, but," I stammered, "I was only going to write down little sentence ideas from them and use them only if I got stuck. I mean, isn't that a fair compromise?"

This dear woman was so patient with me: "Caren, put them back." I put them back, sighed, and looked up at her pleadingly and sadly as she continued. "Now Caren, tie the bag, I mean, really tie the bag." I quietly complied but I clutched my precious bag. She gently and firmly spoke and said, "Now put the bag away, Caren, and thank the papers for how they have already served you in your life." I did what she said.

Suddenly, I remembered Rob at the Java Love Café and how he reaffirmed Tom's approach to our true creative wellspring, the place where we authentically meet ourselves. "This cannot happen, at least not nearly as well, from yesterday's muse," he had explained. He was right! Tom was right! I realized that yesterday's muse is yesterday's news. They both had said also, that if yesterday's news is essential today and we allow ourselves to truly trust in who we are, then it will emerge out of our divine creative selves in the present moment. I felt myself soften, and Valerie smiled.

Just now as I'm writing these words, I hear wedding vows in my head. I realize in that moment with Valerie, I had remarried myself! It was a wedding of joining with my divine self! Yes, I did say, "remarried," because when we arrived on earth as Clarity, pure, unstained, and in a state of knowing, we were married to our true divine selves. As we got chipped away in life, we broke this vow in an amnesic state. Rumi expressed this beautifully, "Even if you have broken your vows a thousand times, come, yet again, come." It is a vow we will break even when we return again. How many times have you been remarried? We never counted because we never realized we had broken the vow.

So, friends, this is not just a personal story about birthing the writer within me. This is a story about self-trust and truly becoming unafraid to meet ourselves along the way. It is a story about coming fully into feelings of adequacy, effectiveness, and self-love.

The small, ego-addicted self lovingly and dutifully tries to rule our world and protect us from every potential hurt along the way. It doesn't realize that once it lets go of itself, the divine, God-connected self will lovingly pull the small, fearful self into the heart and nurture and love that loyal little soldier forever, for all of its beautiful and dutiful intentions. When this happens, the small self can truly return home and experience relief, comfort, and healing.

Think about what would have happened if I had peeked at those pieces of paper. I would have lost trust in myself that I can connect with my divine creative nature, the connection to the source from which we are all derived. I would have short-circuited the pure energy of the divine source and written from a place of trying to recreate. I would have short-changed me, and you. We certainly do not want to be short on "change" for all the hard work we need to do for our souls to not grow sideways. How will we ever reach the light if we only grow sideways?!

It is time to trust that everything we truly need is available to us right here, right now. We must only believe that we are always connected to our divine source. We never need to lean on crutches. Fear makes us want to believe this; it does not want us connecting with our rich divine selves.

So, back to the question posed as the beginning of this chapter: "Why is it so hard for us to return to this sacred place?" As you now understand, it is the collective effect of the oils of our scared small self, an addicted "elf" in fear. It is the ultimate resolution of this fear-based self that sets us free. In love we go to the refinery and return yet again.

Chapter Fourteen

The Story of the Breakthrough Crystal

As we do our soul work to resolve the addicted small self, we begin to see that we have been playing a life game of "spiritual hide-and-seek," where we have been filling the big self, the divine, God-connected self, with the small self. Instead, what we really need to do is fill our fears, insecurities, feelings of inadequacy, and any need to control the world around us with the big self, the divine connected self. We then return fear for self-nurturing and healing. You can always return fear. The only expiration date is your death. You don't need a receipt as you are the proof of purchase. Then when we finally fill our small selves with the clear, crystalline essence that we are, the small self is healed and Clarity returns!

What happens to the powerful and destructive energy that fear houses when it is not resolved? Where does that energy go? I will illuminate this with a recent experience:

I was at a spring equinox celebration weekend in Santa Fe. I was having a fantastic time and learning some amazing things about crystals from Monte Hansen, a man I had met back home in Baltimore. Monte has a deep passion for his work. He feels that he's discovered a very rare and beautiful crystal that may be a connecting clue back to our true origins. I was enjoying the information Monte was sharing and finding it to be very compelling. I was also greatly enjoying all the wonderful people there and connecting with them.

Toward the end of the celebration, and a couple of hours before a beautiful closing ceremony, I received an urgent phone call from Carolyn, the coordinator of the writing retreat I would be attending only a week later. She informed me that my roommate, whom I had never met, was being called out of the country for an emergency, and that I no longer had a roommate for the retreat. By the way she communicated, I chose to feel that she was dumping the problem in my lap and that she was being uncaring. As I shape-shifted with ego-infused judgment, my small self wanted to "tell her like she is."

I shared with a friend at dinner, who was also attending the celebration, and she talked to me about releasing the other person's stuff and staying grounded in the heart. That was very kind of my friend but, of course, it was "my stuff" as it always is for all of us, that I had to release. My small self continued to shape-shift me. "What if I don't get another roommate? I cannot afford this on my own. What if she doesn't help me? Here we go again: no one ever owns their stuff!"

The joke was on me, and I didn't know it. I had now fully shape-shifted, as the grand trickster, Coyote, slipped in on me again. I had a bumper sticker once that said, "Wherever you go, there you are." So true! Hmm, I'd like to create a t-shirt that says, "Your shit, their shit, my shit, no shit!"

We went back to the crystal celebration and I was angry because the closing celebration had already started. I was missing the best part, so I concluded, and justified a heaping portion of indignant cake complete with heavily saturated ego and its fat-filled self. Ego belched and farted, no apologies necessary, left the room with me, and called Carolyn.

Oh dear! Hands on the holsters of my "Two-Gun Tony Set," I left her a message telling her how I thought she had dumped the problem on me and that it was her job to work these issues out. Now, whether this was really true doesn't matter. What matters is that whatever came out of my mouth at that point, even as I self-justified that I had the right to be direct and draw a boundary, was coming from my small addicted self. Remember "self-justification" is one of the negative energy pulls of the addicted self. I did not catch the red flag that Coyote and his overstated ego hid from view. Clearly, I was not grounded in love in the heart.

I came back into the room, my energy noticeably revved up. Hmm, it must have been the "tea" that washed down the cake. In the next moment, I was making a donation to the donation basket for the event, and my jacket hit a beautiful crystal that fell to the floor and broke in half. My heart broke in half right with it as I realized what I had done.

Several participants came over to console me. Monte's wife and his best friend both lovingly said to me, "You are meant to have it." I protested, thinking that it was the last thing I felt worthy of having. His friend explained, "When you break it, it is yours," as he tried to put the broken pieces in my hand. I shared with them how I had just had an experience where I wasn't letting go of judgment. I explained that I was trying to have a controlling effect on another person who I felt was not handling a personal situation right. I continued to say that the last thing I should have is this crystal as a result.

Monte was joyful. He ran over to me and gleefully exclaimed, "I heard it break; I heard it break! I was so happy!"

Confused, I responded, "How can you be happy, Monte? These crystals are like your children. I know how much they mean to you!"

He explained, "Because you had a 'break-through'!" "What "break-through?" I asked sheepishly, still confused. He continued on and explained that negative energy has to go somewhere and is very powerful, so it broke the crystal.

Wow! It was all crystal clear to me now: the shattered crystal shattered my addicted ego's grip. I was jolted into the truth and I was grasping it. Time to get remarried to my true self yet again! So, I went back to the refinery and renewed my wedding vow, the one that says, "Do you, Caren, take your hand to be your lawfully wedded true divine self?" I do, I do!

This was a lesson for me about taking hold of ultimate responsibility for negative emotional energy, because when we don't deal with it and resolve it, it has to go somewhere. Love energy returns to its divine source because it *is* source. Negative emotional energy is *not* source. It is false ego and stays with us, as our responsibility, until we resolve it. If we look a little closer, we can see that in this resolution, it dissipates into the nothingness it really is. It has nothing to do with God. Therefore it has nothing to do with our true selves. It is an illusion.

Meanwhile Monte's friend, Rob, had put the top half of the crystal in my hand. His wife wondered if Monte could put it together. Monte said, "Not necessary. Caren is to have both halves. They are not meant to be put back together, they represent her break-through, and they are broken through. He lovingly handed me the other half and a few shards we found on the ground. He suggested that I take the shards and throw them in the water.

I do want to add that it is never too late to go back when we've lost our grounding in the heart. What would have happened if I had responded to Carolyn from the heart? I think we can all agree that at the very least I would have helped her have a nice day. How quickly people soften when you take your own accountability with them and release them from a hold that was never theirs. Carolyn and I ultimately ended on a very kind and heart-balanced note.

In case any of you believe that I was justified or feel that I was being too hard on myself, remember the true self never needs justifying—only the small self. The more courage we display in facing our own "response-ability," the sooner we rediscover ourselves through re*fining* and end our soul-lesson game of hide-and-go-seek.

We must understand, it is not as important if the words of the message we deliver are faulty. It is more important to understand from which place we deliver them. Do we deliver them from the fear-based, small, addicted self or from the divine, true, heart-connected self? Besides, when we deliver them from the true heart-connected self, the message is never faulty anyway, is it? Can you feel the difference? It is huge... huge!

Even though the example I presented may not be earth-shattering (though, I must admit, it was crystal-shattering), it still matters. All of the necessary lessons are the same, no matter the magnitude of the drama. So, if we say, "Oh, that was just a little one," it gives our scared, ego-addicted selves a toke or a hit, and the next thing you know, it will want another hit and another hit.

Remember with every ripple we send out, even the smallest ripple, we are either healing the world or contributing to war. Is this so overstated? The healing of the world starts with self, always. What ripple do you really want to send out? A small ripple in fear or acting out becomes a hugely detrimental action, if we continue to justify our small false selves. Fear then replicates outward in ever expanding patterns.

A week later, in Sedona, I decided I would release these soul-lesson crystal shards into the beautiful rippling waters of Oak Creek. There is a part of Oak Creek that reflects Cathedral Rock, a vortex energy rock that has become deeply sacred to me. As I stood on the bank of Oak Creek, Cathedral Rock was not directly in view, so I closed my eyes and imagined her sacred stature and essence. I could feel her heart beat with mine. I released the shards into the clear, crystalline, healing waters and felt them being received by her. My comfort returned.

Interlude One—
My Young Writer Inspires Me

The young writer in me encouraged and inspired the next chapter as I began the fourth day of the writer's retreat. Tom invited us, before we started the morning writing session, to connect with our writer within and ask that part of ourselves if there was anything imperative that must be written. I took several grounding, heart-connected breaths, and then I asked and listened:

"You need to tell them what happened. They need to know."

My younger, unstained child writer coaxed me into sharing a painful experience that had just occurred the day before. In the experience, I was confronted with a soul lesson of self-worthiness and of letting love in. I was also confronted, yet again, with a major soul lesson in trust to connect with my divine creative nature. This is the same lesson I came through early that morning when I released my precious pieces of paper. What followed left me so emotionally devastated that I almost could not continue on in the writer's retreat.

So my child writer has lovingly encouraged me to face my grief and deep mourning over the loss, release the painful experience onto paper, give myself a chance to heal further, and not deny you, my dear readers, of the soul lessons to be shared. I felt fear but also the wise truth of my child writer's message as I listened and gulped in acceptance.

Chapter Fifteen

It's Always There, Resolving the Illusion of Lost

Yesterday, I lost 3,000 of the best words I truly felt I had ever written. There is a divine poetry amid the profound grief I felt from what had happened.

I had started that morning at breakfast, releasing the fear of connecting to my divine self and letting go of my sacred precious pearls of paper. I got "remarried," and then joined my fellow writing friends in the morning session. As I began writing that morning, I felt so peaceful and yet elated within myself having just let go to trust my higher creative knowing.

The words were flowing beautifully. I had the sensation of my keyboard becoming a piano. It was as if I was playing it and the words were pouring through me like a channeled melody. I could feel energetic vibrations move up and down my left arm during that morning experience. I wrote as if the words were divine music releasing through me.

Then I finished the morning session writing about soul contracts and the golden chariot, and glanced at my word count as the session was about to end. I had written almost 3,000 words. We had five minutes before the break and I decided to add in one more part. I shared the Hebrew prayer from my childhood of returning to our God-source and saved my document.

Little did I know, I was about to get dished a big slice of soul-lesson pie. Unknown to me, my lesson in trusting my divine creative connection was still not resolved. So, my higher self pulled up in the golden chariot yet again to take me on a jolting ride. I glanced at my word count one more time and then stared in disbelief. Somehow I had lost everything I wrote that morning but the last 152 words. Somehow I had deleted everything else and only saved the last paragraph.

After consulting with one of the writers in the retreat, who happened to be a computer expert, we discovered that either my new word processing program had a bug in it or the default function was not set to save the document history. I may have accidentally highlighted the document unknown to me and deleted it. Holding on to a glimmer of hope, I carried my computer and its lost document like a stillborn child, as I cried across the parking lot and into the doors of a computer recovery group. They could not save my baby. I was so grief-stricken and faced with having to accept that what I felt was my best writing ever, had evaporated in an instant—poof!

When I came back to the room, having returned from the computer recovery group, I met over thirty loving writing friends who tried to comfort me in kind words and caring support. I felt unconditional love and great understanding from them. Some told me I was not meant to write those words and that greater would come. I thanked them, as I secretly wept in pain, not accepting this to be the reason for the soul lesson. I tried to deal with the reality of my situation and clear my head to write but I was an emotional mess.

As our world of meaningful coincidences would have it, my scheduled session for myofascial release was upon me. This was an energy-balancing and clearing opportunity that Tom had set up for us as an optional support in connecting with our "Creative Connected Mind," as Tom calls it. Myofascial release helps the participant release old, stored, and stuck energy in order to gain clearer access to our true selves and release our emotional holdings, even the ones we don't know we still have. I had decided two days prior to take advantage of it, not knowing when my session time would come. I had not even been sitting down two minutes and the practitioner came in to get me. My session time came in that exact moment as if orchestrated by divine intervention, my higher self serving as the conductor. So with the orchestra in the background of my opera, I practically fell into the arms of Elaina, my practitioner. I felt like a part of my soul had been cut out of me, as I felt I would never be able to get that divine, source-connected feeling in my writing ever again—at least not to that degree. I felt as if a deeply connected part of me had been amputated.

Elaina and Tom insisted that I must release the anguish. Elaina strategically worked with my energy while Tom urged me to move through it so that I could clear the pained emotional energy and reconnect with my source once again. I resisted. "I can't. They will hear me, I can't let it out. The walls are too thin. They are all writing—I cannot disturb them."

Tom playfully interjected, "Don't worry, Caren, they are all too self-absorbed to notice." I almost chuckled as he chipped a piece of fear out of me. Still, I was so afraid to make room for me and be willing to make myself valuable enough to give me what I knew I most needed.

I was familiar with similar kinds of emotional release work and how it can very quickly move one to the core and origin of any related pain. I did not want to bring up old, stored energy, not with all of my writing colleagues in the next room. If I was a toddler, I would have been stomping my feet with "not gonna, not gonna, can't make me, can't make me" iterations. Besides, I had done my share of "release work" over the years as a faithful student of healing practices. I am supposed to be past all of this stuff, right? Refinery, schminery!

I dug my feet in, as they encouraged me toward the massage table that felt like the edge of a cliff to my scared self. My higher self beckoned, inviting me to go deeper as the golden chariot pulled up to my side. My scared self relented and dug my energy into the ground. Elaina had her arms around my torso trying to move my energy, Tom urged me on, and finally I belted out one very audible and stretched out "fuuuuuuuuck," followed by another belting, "I didn't come here to do this!"

Then I felt my energy shift just a bit, and I said, "Oh, yes, I did," and I chuckled just a little as I started to win that round of psycho-spiritual hide-and-go-seek. Guided by my higher self and finally releasing my fear, I knew in the middle of belting it out that I must have come here to do this or I would not be doing it, so I chuckled for a moment and so did they. I also quickly knew to stay in the process and honor what needed to be released.

Old emotional traumas from my life came flooding back into my consciousness where people lost in negativity had attempted to steal power from me, manipulate me, blame me for their stuff, and most of all thwart my efforts to be my best self. Somehow, I was in the middle of the perfect dive in my greatest essence and someone came and cut my dive off.

They did not let me complete the experience when I was finally ready. I have many times been at my highest peak and felt cut off. This one is a soul lesson for me, and my golden chariot came right in the middle of the writer's retreat, driven by my loving higher self with its GPS system programmed for "1 Soul Contract Road," destination "Earth School."

My higher self lovingly beckoned me to go further in my soul contract lessons, step in and honor this sacred process. I knew I had to succumb. I had to give it room because this is what we do when we are learning to fall back in love with ourselves. And so I did. I went deeper into lessons of self-valuing. I gave myself the sacred room to do my emotional releasing, even knowing that others would hear (yup, naked is a good thing)! I am now a member of the psycho-spiritual nudist community. Membership is freeing! And so another day at the refinery is complete.

So, dear readers, nothing is ever lost. It is impossible to lose our essence. We may lose our way temporarily, but we can never lose our essence because it is infinitely and forever connected to the divine source from which we are derived. Can you get from this the importance of honoring your work, the work of your soul? These are the lessons we all came here to complete that our divine, loving source will undyingly present to us over and over in loving commitment.

Our divine, loving source yearns for our return. Like a divine mother, she unconditionally holds her outstretched arms to receive us and nurture us out of the grip of fear. Symbolically, Elaina was like that divine mother, as I had fallen into her arms terrified and she held me in this sacred process. This is a beautiful journey. This is a beautiful day.

When I came back from the myofascial release session to rejoin my fellow writing friends, who were vehemently writing away, I shook off my concerns that they had heard me and my fear that I had interrupted their process. I returned to the room unashamed, feeling strong and resolved, and accepting that I made the space to do what was necessary at that time. My fellow writing journey mates were quietly working, and I sat down to recommence.

One by one, several of my writing friends came over to me. I received their hugs and became overwhelmed by the depth of love, concern, and compassion they offered. One friend, Angelique, gave me a most heartfelt gift, a beautiful angel with heart-shaped wings in a clear encasement with an accompanying poem to keep for comfort and protection. She told me she had stopped writing to say an angel prayer for me when she realized what had happened. Her name suited her; she exuded such unconditional angelic energy.

Another woman, Victoria, who had led our Resonance Repatterning before the retreat, offered me healing oils for transformation, calming, and comfort. She continued to offer this to me for the rest of the retreat. Several people actually told me they were inspired because I was continuing. One fellow writer said that if I could continue writing with what I had just been through, then he certainly could finish his book. I was beaming from taking in the love of these beautiful people.

Tom got up in front of the class and shared what most of them knew by then, that I had lost 3,000 words of my writing that morning, that what many of us had feared the most had come true for me. He congratulated me for my courage to bravely do the emotional work of releasing my grief and stated to the group that I was back to continue.

Everyone clapped loudly for me. Tears welled in my eyes and my heart opened even more. I wasn't used to such a magnitude of love expressed for me. I had no idea the impact I had on the others and was overjoyed with love.

I stood up and told them something that I had directly felt while moving through my grief work next door: "We are all truly brilliant, beautiful, and amazing!" I told them that this was not about me but about all of us, our greatness, and our willingness to embrace ourselves on such an honest and pure level in order to do our writing, in order to do this work of our souls. I thanked them for our shared journey and experience and told them how I felt we were all part of a unified energy of manifestation, receiving such deep support from each other in this collective experience.

Three thousand words was actually a very small price to pay for the powerful soul lessons I had received. One is that I am worthy of love. I went deeper in this life lesson that all of us are here resolving. Any insecurity that we carry in this lifetime reflects this unresolved lesson. The love that comes from others is only a reflection of our own selves. And so, my dear readers, let the love in! Please do not deny the love that comes to you from others or you will only be denying yourself who you are. And you are beautiful and deserving and radiant light. The overwhelming and uplifting love from all of my writing friends took me even deeper into this lesson.

The other lesson I received (at that moment I did not integrate it, but as I continued on in my writing I have learned it) is that the only thing any of us can ever lose is that which is not divinely connected. This can only be tied to original addiction and it originates in the earthly realms, so it is *scared*, not *sacred*. What we must actually lose are the fears that live within the small self. So for a very small price of 3,000 words, I released fear into my heart where it rested in divine connection for relief, healing, and love.

What I thought I lost in divine connection was never really lost. You cannot ever lose something that is divinely connected because divinity is infinite! So, losing 3,000 words could never take me away from who I truly am. You can never lose what is intrinsically yours. You may confuse your confidence in staying in touch, but you can never lose an infinite God connection.

It is part of who you are! Your inner creative brilliance is derived from your divine nature. Your true nature is a bottomless cup that never ceases to fill from the oneness of which we are all essentially a part.

Interlude Two—
My Young Writer Rejoices

The next morning, Tom had us connect again with our young writer within. I checked in with her and this is what she said:

"Hey, I'm excited. We got this! We are really together now."

I noticed her arms were happily "flailing."

I call it "flailing" and this is a really good thing. It comes with a buzzy kind of energy when creative expression is at a peak. I know it myself in my present-day life. The first time I felt it, I was in a metal sculpture class. With the help of my teacher, we successfully pulled off a tricky process with the metal on a very personally meaningful sculpture. I felt such joy and excitement that I hooted out loud, involuntarily, since it came right from my divine connected spirit, and my arms started flailing, flapping up and down.

So now I felt and saw my young writer happily flapping. I never thought about how she knew this feeling, too. I connected with her joy and exuberant passion for expressing creatively and stopped writing so I could flap, too. Think "happy chicken." I don't know if it was her or I that decided to call this the "happy chicken." I think we are coming together more and more. I stopped writing to flap and flail with her. We do the "chicken dance," except we've renamed it, "the liberated chicken dance!"

Chapter Sixteen

Creative Divinity

I invite you now to think about a time when you were feeling a deeper, truer connection to yourself. It could be through art or anything creative. Any true connection to yourself by definition is "creative" because God is the ultimate creator. When you are in touch with your God-connected self, your truest relation to yourself, you are in your highest, most pure creative state.

Think about a time when you felt this pure connection. Feel the creative energy that was moving through your body at the time. What was happening in your body? What were your thoughts doing? What were you feeling? What did your energy feel like?

If you are not feeling it yet, please do not be so quick to say that you never had such an experience. Breathe, and get grounded. Intentional breathing will help you do this. Most of the time, you are only five conscious deep breaths away from your divine true self. Yes, only five breaths of separation that we often treat as a gulf. Resolve this illusion and breeaathe...

For some of you, as you connect, you may find yourself going back to a more uninhibited time in childhood to re-experience this pure creative state. Some of you may have a more recent memory come up, which is certainly to be honored as well. But I encourage you to connect even further with that much younger part of yourself—the one that first experienced this creative energy that carries the blueprint of who you truly are. You will know you are connecting this way because it will bring a feeling of perfection, as if everything is exactly as it is meant to be. You will feel free of judgment, and very present and receptive in this memory of yourself.

Some of you are feeling this now as you connect. For others, you will need to be patient; be kind to yourself and love yourself, as you may have been long out of touch with this pure, creative energy. You may think of a time in childhood when you felt the most uninhibited and free within yourself— this will help you connect.   Put this book down for a moment and breathe, reconnect, and remember… Did you put the book down? If you did not, please do this now; you deserve to take the space for you. Breathe, be patient, and be receptive; breathe in your life, breathe in you, and reconnect….

As you look back in childhood and re-experience this pure connection to yourself, it may show up as a moment when you were dancing in a recital, or even just freely playing in your childhood home with a friend, or peacefully alone in your room. It may come up as you recall acting in a play and expressing yourself with your heart. It may come up in a million ways when you simply played, or maybe you were singing. Go ahead, try it again, feel it again, go deeper if you already got there, or just give yourself a chance again if you have not felt it yet.

Creativity is part of the birthright from which we came. It has to be because it only knows its source. It is of our divine source. It is a sense of unabashed, uninhibited connection. Love comes with it; it *is* love. Pure, divine creativity is love. That's why we go back to childhood to feel it, because we have not had as much time for the conditioning and oil spills to set in. We are, by nature, more directly connected with our divine source because we have not yet lived long enough to weaken that connection. Be with this reconnection and your memory of it as long as you are guided to do so.

If you are not yet feeling the conscious, creative connection that ultimately takes you back to your birth self, Clarity, just know that at some point you may have stopped believing that she was really there. This is only an illusion born of oil spills that clouded your view. You can never not be connected to the creative source because it is who you really, really are! God created you and that is amazingly creative and miraculous! Since you are a microcosm of God, you have God's blueprint. That is who you are, so you are creative just like your creator!

Now, for those of you who have experienced childhood trauma, please know that you are loved and give yourself a hug. Take a moment and allow yourself to connect with compassion to that child part of you that was hurt. If this exercise has connected you with despair, please know that trauma can sometimes block creative energy. However, since we are all unique in the way we adapt in the world, not all of you became blocked. Some of you who have been through childhood trauma may have actually deepened your connection to creative source energy as a means to emotionally survive the trauma. In both cases I honor you and your bravery, I honor your perseverance. I honor you for surviving the pain of whatever your beautiful self was subjected to.

Even negative and harsh judgmental messages from a parent or guardian figure are a form of trauma. This is because when someone on whom you depended for your survival told you that you were bad, unworthy, inadequate, or blamed you in any way for their bad day, that sliced right through your creative, loving core. You then began the process of self-denial.

Self-denial means denial of your true brilliant crystalline full-spectral self, reflected in your original name, Clarity. In self-denial, you began to lose Clarity. It was not your fault. Remember that and really let that in! It was not your fault. Love yourself because it is never too late. Begin now.

I will take a moment to address those of you who have undergone a severing of this most essential umbilical cord to your divine, creative Clarity. Please know, it was never really severed, it just felt that way because of the traumas you have survived. Even for those of you with no such feeling of severing, remember that each and every one of us is in recovery of ourselves. To the extent that we are in spiritual amnesia, we are in recovery.

No one is exempt, as we are all in a lifetime journey of re-calling who we truly are. We go to the refinery every day to do this. We must always honor our recovery and all of its needs, for it is the most sacred aspect of our earthly journey. In es-sence, it is the very reason that you are here. Since you have God's blueprint, you just want to know your God self better. Feel that and feel who you are. Feel you and your beautiful, awesome, God-loving light.

I want to offer you a meditation to reconnect this essential cord of life. This is a guided meditation for each and every one of you—even if you are able to connect with your creative source, please join in this guided meditation. It can only serve to deepen and strengthen your creative connection even more. Please refer to the box below entitled, "Cord of Life," to do this meditation. Like the other guided imagery meditations in this book, this is available on my website, *www.ultimate-healing.com*, as an audio download for your ease of meditating.

CORD OF LIFE

I want you to imagine a ball of bright golden light above your head and, as you breathe, this bright golden ball of light is moving downward. With each breath notice and feel this ball of light moving into you, first into your crown chakra. Breathe this in a few times and, when you are ready, feel this ball move into your third eye. Now, breathe this in a few times. When you are ready, feel it move downward into your throat chakra and breathe this in a few times. This golden bright ball of light continues to move downward, and you now notice and feel it moving down into your heart chakra. Breathe this in and notice what you are feeling.

This ball of bright golden light is your divine self moving through you, through all of your energies and expressions of yourself, and reconnecting to you at every level of your expressed being. Breathe this in...breeaathe...and get ac-quainted with the essence of your divine self. What are you feeling as you experience this true connection? Your divine self is always connected to the divine source, and it is who you really are.

Now imagine this bright golden ball of light moving down into your solar plexus and breathe and notice whatever you feel and see. Take in any colors, sounds, or temperatures you are experiencing. When you are ready, move this sacred golden ball of your divine-connected self down into your belly and breathe; notice whatever you feel and see. Next move your beautiful, bright, golden light-infused ball into your root chakra, and breathe this in and notice what you feel and see—including any colors, sounds, or temperatures you are experiencing—as you fill yourself with your true divine essence.

Now, as this divine golden ball sits in your root chakra, I want you to shift your focus to the infinite cosmos of which we are a part. When you are connected with that feeling, I want you to imagine another bright golden ball of light way, way up high in the cosmos—as high as you can imagine. This ball of golden bright light is surrounded by divine light beings. Some of you may experience them as angels. Just know however you see them, they are divine and loving guardians of the light, and they are surrounding this divine golden ball of light as they love and assist you. Imagine these loving beings of light and notice how many of them you see? What do they look like? However many you see and how they appear to you is exactly right for you.

Imagine they are breathing into this beautiful, golden ball of light and, as they continue to do that, a magnificent, vibrant cord of light begins to descend out of the golden ball. They are assisting in this, for as they breathe into the ball, this light-infused cord continues to get longer and longer and begins to descend down from the heavens.

This cord is actually God's consciousness. It reaches for you because you are an extension of this God-loving consciousness and the pure love of divinity always wants itself. So, it descends to earth and is heading toward you and your root chakra, where your golden ball of light awaits the arrival of this divine, God-conscious umbilical cord of light. Keep breathing as you feel this cord of light connecting to your golden ball of light. As this connection happens, notice this vibrant cord of light is now infused with every color of the spectrum flowing through it as pure, crystalline, full-spectral energy. Keep breathing and notice as this full spectral energy of light fills your root chakra and mingles with the golden light of your divine self. Breathe this in, breeaathe... and notice whatever you are feeling.

Next this full spectrum of light begins to expand upward from your root chakra. You feel it fill into your belly. Then it continues to expand upward into your solar plexus, then to your heart chakra, and then it expands further into your throat chakra. Take your needed time; breathe and notice it now filling all the way to your third eye and up to meet your crown. Breathe and feel yourself filled with the divine, crystalline, full-spectral, God-conscious light that you are. Feel it mingling with your earth blood and circulating through your system. Breathe and relax, breathe and feel, breathe and take in. Feel all there is for you to feel in the moment. Know that you are truly a child of God and that you are and always will be God-connected.

Welcome home, Clarity. Stay here for as long as you choose and be present.

Did you know that this moment is a gift? That's why it is called "the present!" You were never severed after all. This divinely connected cord is always there and, whenever you feel any sense of disconnection, you can return to this cord. You do not necessarily have to recreate the whole meditation. You can just imagine a connected cord of light from the cosmos to your root chakra. Then imagine the cord infused with a pure, crystalline, full-spectral light and filling all throughout you. The angels and beings of light are smiling with great feelings of love for you. Fill your heart with their song breath as you awaken to your creative self.

Chapter Seventeen

You are Fractal in Nature

G od wants more of God, and this relates to your process of awakening into your divine source. Even those on an unconscious path are moving toward this divine outcome, the truth of our journey toward recovery of our God-connected selves. We simply choose individually when we consciously wake up into it.

A beautiful example of this energy lies in fractals. Have you heard of fractals? What is this strange term? In this chapter, I will share what I have learned from many years of studying fractals to help you in your understanding.[15] Fractals are re-peated patterns of self-similarity, from the micro levels of our existence to the macro—kind of like a divine blueprint.

Fractals repeat their essence on infinite levels in never-end-ing patterns that can be measured with mathematics. They are a beautiful example of love wanting to become more and more of itself, of our divine source seeking itself and inventing itself. In fact, they never stop evolving and expressing themselves. They are timeless and are always in a state of becoming. They have no beginning or end—they are a definition of infinity.

Infinity is complete, unconditional love. But it can't really complete itself because in its loving state, it wants to become more and more of itself. It can be said that infinity is God. God wants to know more of God and doesn't want to miss any possibilities. He doesn't want to miss an aspect of himself. There is no end. That is the nature of our universe, of God and, therefore, of you. What would happen if you wanted to become more and more of yourself? This is why I am explaining fractals to you as a most beautiful and perfect expression of self-love and divinity. They are the visualization of divine creation. We are fractal in our infinite nature. This is a way to understand ourselves on the deepest and purest level.

I am so compelled by fractals because the more I study them, the more I feel that they are a reflection of our true selves as one connected source with our infinite, beautiful expressions. I wrote a poem reflecting this great truth of our oneness entitled, "Kaleidoscope (A Fractal Poem of Oneness)":

I am reflected—
the terms of my environment
define my portrayal.

Same reflects different and then to same.
A thousand and more times—this happens.
And the colors and forms collide and rebound
their faces and names.

I am here and there,
there or here and here...
Specks-connected-to-the-whole.
I am a snowflake on a delicately fragile day
or the radiant sun in my light.
I am a dot of God—
in a mirror, I may magnify large or small.

Reflection has its truth and illusions—
it just depends on where you live.

Gaze into your scope and find its riddle.
You could be bored or content to discover
that each portrayal gives you infinitely back to yourself.
It just depends on where you live.

Are you one-and-all or all-for-one
or none at all or me or you?

Fractals teach us a very important lesson about our divine nature, since they reflect who we are. A fractal doesn't get caught up in its story. It doesn't say, "Hey, look at me, I'm ugly," or "I'm great." It just *does*. And then it becomes more and more of itself. If a fractal got caught in its story, it would cease to self-perpetuate. That's like saying if infinity got caught up in itself, it would cease to self-perpetuate and then there would be no infinity. All of life would cease. So, fractals teach us about our divine flow. In a sense, when we get caught up in our stories, we cease to exist, since the small self is not real. Only our divine, God-connected, fractal, infinite selves are real.

Fractals are derived from mathematical equations of infinity. What we see in fractals are smaller images repeating themselves as larger images. Images in fractals seem to get smaller and smaller as if they are disappearing into infinity, or larger and larger as if they are exploding into infinity. The whole is in the part and the part is in the whole—or, more aptly, the whole is in the heart and the heart is in the whole, because fractals are actually expressions of divine love. Can you see through fractals the implication that we are microcosms of God? We might even say we are a microcosm of the entire universe. Fractals, in their visual patterns, reflect this truth.

I invite you to imagine, via your intuition, what a fractal image might look like. Go ahead. Give yourself a chance to do this. All of the knowledge of existence lives within you— there is no separation. Remember. To help you with this, imagine if you could take a snapshot of infinity. What would it be like to take a snapshot of something that goes on and on and does not seem to have a beginning or an end? Hmm.... what do you see? I am sure you are getting a piece of this as you tap in. Consider that infinity represents every possible expression and every possible outcome. What are you seeing in this snapshot of infinite possibilities? Can any two snapshots be exactly alike?

Continue visualizing via your intuition and sense of knowing. What are you seeing now? I guarantee you that whatever you are visualizing is fractal in nature. It would not be unexpected that you are all getting different images, but there would be no doubt that you are all tapping into an experience of fractals. Know that your fractal image is already perfect and right. There is a double meaning in what I just said, because you yourself are fractal in nature. I will explain further.

You see fractal patterns show up on every level of life. Makes sense, right? Since they are infinite in their expression, they would have to show up on every level of life, from the microcosmic to the macrocosmic. These patterns show up in a repeated ratio that has become known as the divine ratio. Here is something awesome: fractal ratios show up in the very structure of our DNA!

On another level, the emotional ripples we send out have a fractal quality; their energetic vibration repeats on every level of our lives and reflects this pattern of self-similarity. Fractal patterns even show up in our bodies as ratios of the distance between different body parts—for example the ratio of hand size to forearm length. Their ratios also show up on earth in the patterns of pine cones as they spiral up toward their top, as well in the spiral of the nautilus shell, and even in the center of a sunflower as its pattern moves toward the center. In our planet's atmosphere, fractal patterns show up in storm funnel spirals and hurricanes. Beyond that, their ratio patterns show up even in the Milky Way, in the pattern of other galaxies, and in the orbits of certain planets.

Some of the highly creative, connected beings that have walked our earth seem to have had an understanding of fractals.

For example, in a fractal analysis of the paintings of Leonardo da Vinci, mathematicians have discovered proportional ratios in his paintings of people that exactly equal the divine proportional ratio of fractals. In addition, the pyramids in Egypt and their geometry are said to contain this same divine ratio.

This divine ratio is known as the Golden Mean Ratio and is also known as Phi. For reference, its number is 1.618. It is a number derived from something called the Fibonacci series. The Fibonacci series is a series of numbers in a sequence. When you divide one number in the sequence into the one before it, the division between those numbers equals the Golden Mean Ratio over and over. It cannot escape itself. Infinity does not want to escape itself. God does not want to escape God! A very interesting point is that in the Golden Mean Ratio, while it stabilizes in its first several digits, the other digits of the ratio are never exact. They never approach a point of exact sameness because infinity—you guessed it—never stops knowing and discovering more of itself. Sounds like God, right? Sounds like us, right?

Earlier, when you were imagining what a fractal would look like, I explained that your fractal image is already perfect and right. You are already perfect and right. You are fractal in nature. Fractals are a direct representation of your divine blueprint. We are all internal artists of fractals as we create and evolve ourselves in our infinite possible expressions. We become more of who we are as we reach for our divinity that never ends.

We seem to respond to fractals on a deep subconscious level of knowing. You can meditate while gazing at fractal images to bring yourself into deeper brainwave states. Studies done at The University of Oregon showed that just spending time gazing at fractal images increases feelings of well-being and peace and increases the size of one's aura field.[16] Many people have reported experiencing fractal images during deep brainwave states and even during near death experiences.

If you search fractals on the Internet, you will get treated further to these divine cosmic images; there are many fractal websites to explore should you desire to delve further. I am so utterly intrigued by fractals that I have become a fractal artist and have dedicated some time into creating these "snapshots" for others to enjoy. The cover on this book is one example of a fractal that I created. On my website, *www.ultimate-healing.com*, you can purchase my photo book on fractals. There is also a link to a gallery page of my fractals for purchase.

I will share a brief story before we leave this divinely magical subject of fractals. I was invited to do a coffeehouse show of my fractal images; I was, of course, very excited to do this. As it was my first show, I didn't have a notion of what to expect but I was hoping that the viewers would connect with these images more than superficially. I was tremendously rewarded. People greeted me at the door with comments like, "There she is. She's the fractal artist. Hey, I want to talk to her..." What they were all eager to share was what they felt when they looked at the images. Each in their own words, they described a sense of serenity, calm, and peacefulness, yet they found themselves energized. Many of them said they did not really understand how the images were making them feel that way but that they were feeling so wonderful in the presence of them. I am currently in the beginning of another fractal show at the same coffeehouse, and I look forward to the continued connections and experiences people will have as they gaze at these snapshots from the infinite source of which they are a part.

Chapter Eighteen

The Hundredth Monkey and the Maharishi Effect

L et us go further into our magical divine universe and this fantastic earth that each of us, on a soul level, has signed up to participate in. I want to talk about the "Hundredth Monkey Phenomenon." For those of you aware of what this is, please enjoy a brief review of this amazing phenomenon. This version of the phenomenon comes from the book, *Lifetide*, by Lyall Watson.[17] The phenomenon was discovered on the Japanese island of Koshima.

In 1952 scientists were dropping sweet potatoes in the island sand to feed the monkeys. As they observed the monkeys, they noticed one of them started washing her potatoes in the nearby water, and then taught her mother. Soon the scientists observed other monkeys catching on. By 1958 all the young monkeys were washing their potatoes in the water, and adults who imitated their children did so, too. Then an amazing thing happened. As if a critical mass had been reached, all of a sudden in one evening, all of the remaining monkeys on the island started washing their potatoes.

Though the exact number preceding this spontaneous mass learning was not known, it became known as the "Hundredth Monkey Phenomenon." The story goes even further. This habit of washing the potatoes then crossed the sea, as monkey colonies on neighboring islands and on the nearby mainland began washing their potatoes, too! Those monkeys began assimilating the same utilitarian change though they had never before seen it.

This reminds me of the energy of spontaneous combustion where a fire spreads ever so slowly until the intensity has reached a critical mass and spontaneously explodes into a roar. This hundredth monkey effect is a powerful implication of how we are divinely connected by the ripple effect. You can see that it goes beyond emotions into our very behaviors as illustrated with the monkeys on Koshima.

I would surmise, however, that the emotional aspect is essential as a connecting force and catalyst for the mass change. The first monkey on the original island was likely to feel elated at her discovery, "Hey look at this wonderful new way of enjoying potatoes without having to eat the sand." This sent out a ripple effect that increased to the point of hitting a critical mass, at which time the growing conscious energy wave exploded into the consciousness of nearby neighboring monkeys. The emotional aspect is the driving engine, without which there would not likely have been such a mass effect. Recall to mind that the research from the Institute of HeartMath demonstrated the heart's electromagnetic field can transmit information below consciousness between people. Why not monkeys? So, *monkey feel, monkey do!*

What quality of ripple do you want to create and send? You may be the hundredth monkey. No matter what, you will be part of the energy that builds toward its spontaneous combustion. Did you ever think that our very thoughts are as powerful as nuclear energy? Can you see how they have the power to sustain, evolve, devolve, or destroy us?

What if the monkeys on the first island were really an unhappy bunch who had no clue about their divine monkey natures? What if they argued and fought and came from a point of view of scarcity and fear and rudely started beating each other up with the sweet potatoes? Besides there being a lot of bruised potatoes and a lot of bruised monkeys, the monkeys on the other island would have been susceptible to getting very *faklempt* (Yiddish for flustered and choked with emotion) as they bruised each other and their potatoes as well. What an unkind thing for these divine, loving, sentient monkeys to do to themselves and their nice sweet potatoes.

What an unkind thing to do to the divine, loving, sentient beings that we are, too! Let's stop bruising each other with potatoes or the many other ways we might invent to bruise each other. We are utterly responsible for each other; it is our responsibility to ourselves to recognize this. Be kind to your fellow monkey and choose the energy of your ripples wisely. Know with all your heart—as I am sure you are beginning to grasp this point—that you are a divinely powerful human being who can create your personal universe and ultimately the collective universe as you so choose.

In order to further demonstrate in a similar way the far-reaching effects of our choices, here is another related example of our shared grid of life and how we intimately affect each other. Like the Hundredth Monkey Phenomenon illustrates, this next example, known as the "Maharishi Effect," also shows us how divinely powerful we really are. It is a fantastic illustration of the effect of our ripples when we send out positive energy through meditation.

Many independent studies have been done to demonstrate this effect, which is created through transcendental meditation (TM). TM was originated by Maharishi Mahesh Yogi over fifty years ago and has been known to transform the lives of many. Researchers were able to empirically show that TM can be a powerful catalyst for spontaneous mass change when only a few are practicing it. They were able to show that when 1 percent of a population practices Maharishi's Transcendental Meditation program, the collective energy of that population begins to synchronize into a unified force that yields measurable positive mass change. In other words, individual consciousness clearly affects mass consciousness.

One such study was conducted in Rhode Island.[18] Sufficient participants to produce the effect for the entire state came in and practiced TM. Their job was solely to initiate their normal daily transcendental meditation practice for a three-month period. A monthly time-series analysis assessed the quality of life in Rhode Island and was compared to a demographically matched control state.

The results were undeniable and amazing. During the experimental period, the following variables significantly decreased: crime, motor vehicle fatalities, auto accidents, deaths, alcoholic beverage and cigarette consumption, unemployment, and pollution. A number of other studies have also demonstrated significant effects on the quality of life in an entire nation, using the same mathematical parameters to produce the effect.

Do you see how beautifully we change the world when we change the inner world within ourselves? Do you get the magnitude of the implication for healing on all levels? Can you get that one person can truly change the world? Through the examples of the Hundredth Monkey Phenomenon and the Maharishi Effect, this can now have tangible meaning for you. With both stories, we strongly see the astounding power of our ripples and how we create our universe accordingly. Take this in to your heart and feel the beautiful beat of your individual rippling power!

Chapter Nineteen

Sister Grace and her 'Saving Graces'

L et's dive even deeper into our ripples to understand what ultimately happens when they are generated out of fear. There is a beautiful implication here about our ripples. A love-infused ripple is in harmony with God and is in alignment with our true God-connected self. It goes on forever, as it is already complete, so it joins with God's infinity. But a ripple infused with the energy of fear would be oil-spilled; God lovingly gives us these ripples back to clean up. So, our fear-based ripples enter into a loving feedback loop from God, where God sends them back to us for clean up and transformation. This is because of the nature of God's essence; God can only exist as love.

Now, if you want to know what your thoughts and ripples are doing, just look at the world around you. If you don't like your world around you, change your thoughts and thereby change your ripples. Of course, that means changing your emotional relationship to your thoughts.

To accomplish this, we must return the small, scared, thought-addicted self, who meant so much to us, to our hearts, for nurturing and healing. It is important that we thank this small self ever so lovingly for being dedicated and working so hard to protect our world. We must then nurture this small, pained self out of its fear through patient and loving acknowledgment. We are then able to shift our locus of relating to being grounded in love in the heart with the pure loving essence that our divine big self really is. Through this, we then fill the world with our birth name, Clarity.

Now, Clarity has a loving sister named Grace and it is time to introduce her. Grace is like the strong Hindu goddess, Kali, who will not spare a lesson, no matter how painful, for the sake of resolving ourselves fully into love. Though fiercely loving, she brings temperance along the way so that we can endure and assimilate our powerful lessons. Sister Grace comes during our more difficult soul lessons, during our more traumatic life experiences. She allows Clarity the time to find herself by bringing such lessons with compassion. Grace reminds us that even in the trauma of traumas there is a higher meaning, even though pain confuses us out of this truth at times. Grace allows us to honor and move through our soul lessons and not become stuck in the fearing small self. Grace brings along smaller "saving graces" in her love for us as we move through these more traumatic soul lessons. I will tell you a story of Sister Grace and her "saving graces."

In 1990, I had just bought my first home. Two loving felines, named Oreo and Tux, and I moved into our new beautiful home excited and happy. I lived in a condominium called "Fireside" and all of the units had fireplaces (Yes, that's a hint of the story, but bear with me as I unfold what lessons I brought into my life at the time). About three months into living at my new home, I planned a day out with my five-year-old niece, Heidi, whom I love very much.

I had only used the fireplace a handful of times—I had not grown up in a home with a fireplace. That morning, I decided that I needed to clean out the ashes in the fireplace from the night before. It had been about ten hours since I had snuffed out the fire and I noticed the grey, dead ashes. I proceeded to sweep out the grey dead ashes with my little fireplace broom, all the while watching for embers just to make sure they were all grey and dead.

Convinced that they were as I carefully swept, I balled the

ashes into newspaper and proceeded to throw them into the kitchen trash can. After all, they were grey and dead. I almost caught what was about to happen, but this was not to be. I was about to learn my first conscious lesson by Grace. I thought to myself, "Gee, these ashes smell strong; can ashes smell strong?" I pondered this as I sorted through mail and dumped kindling onto the fire that was about to start. Grace would not have me linger as I had to go pick up my niece for our day out. And so I departed, unaware at the time that my kitchen trash can was smoldering.

I had mentioned to my sister-in-law that we were going to the National Aquarium in Washington, D.C. (I lived in the D.C. suburbs at that time), among other places. We arrived at the aquarium a few hours later and, while we were in there, a woman appeared walking around the aquarium with a clipboard. She inquired aloud, "Is there a Caren Appel in here?" My heart skipped a beat as I said, "Yes, I am Caren Appel." She told me that there had been an emergency and that my brother was on the phone.

Of course, all the obvious and scary thoughts raced through my mind as she ushered me and my niece into the aquarium office. It is interesting to me now that aquariums represent water and that I was standing in the middle of a very large one, with divine Sister Grace, about to receive the news from my brother of the fire. This feels to me now like Grace providing her first saving grace, a counter-balancing of the elements to help me deal with the huge emotional energy from the trauma that was about to unfold.

With my five-year-old niece by my side, I took the phone and heard my brother say to me, "Caren, there has been a fire and you need to come home with Heidi now." I responded, "How bad, Larry?" He minimized it and responded, "Well, it was mostly the kitchen." Right away, I realized what had started the fire and told him.

Funny, my brother is a volunteer fireman and emergency medical technician, and I will tell you now about this wonderful soul that I am so fortunate to have chosen for a brother. He has been there for me unconditionally in my life. In the life moments that have been particularly overwhelming, where I lost my balance and was not getting back to a grounded self easily on my own, my brother has always been there to help me put out my fires of fear. He is a man who has also dedicated his life to helping many others put out their fires of fear as a medical professional and simply as the unconditionally caring person that he is. He is, in fact, a saving grace in my life.

In denial, I responded, "Well, since it's only in the kitchen, and Dad is a cabinet maker, I will just spend the day out with Heidi and see you later as planned. Dad can make me new cabinets and all will be fine." With my emotional buffers blocking the coming pain, I could not let in the implications. Larry continued, "Well, the fire marshal wants to speak with you." I said, "Oh, well, then I guess I have to come home." My dear protective brother wanted to make sure Heidi and I got home safely, of course.

On the way home, Heidi kept saying, "Aunt Caren, I hope your cats are okay."

"Oh, honey," I said, "They are fine. It was just a small fire." A look of concern never left her beautiful, pure face. As a young child, she was so much more divinely connected and unstained in her intuition than me. She could read the energy that I could not.

We pulled into the condo complex, I immediately smelled the stench and finally got the magnitude of destruction that the fire had burned into my life. Instantly, the reality I had shunned, blasted in. As I pulled up to the condo, my neighbor greeted me with a look of tremendous loving concern. She said, "The firemen took one of your cats to the animal hospital." I realized right away that the other cat had died in the fire.

You may be asking, where is Grace in all of this? Remember, Grace, like Kali, brings our lessons, even fiercely, but only because of love and her desire for us to heal and return to Clarity. I cannot say that the soul lessons of this fire are entirely known to me. There are times when we must move on after taking in whatever value we are able. What I do know, however, is that there were lessons on how to deal with trauma and feelings of victimization as I moved through the pain of the experience. I also know that there were lessons of self-forgiveness to be learned as I released self-blame.

I will begin with a correlation of timing and its related meaningful implications. You see, at that time in my life I was moving through feelings of emotional confusion from a vague sense of a repressed unsettling childhood memory. I was also moving through resulting depression energy as I attempted to release anger I didn't fully understand. At that young adult age, sometimes it felt like a deep internal inferno burning within me that I did not know how to extinguish, especially because I did not understand its properties. In the experience of the fire, I had to learn how to move through trauma. Perhaps this was to help me move through other emotional trauma in my life at the right time.

I was involved in conscious psycho-spiritual practices, but I was still coming from my small self's fear and victimhood. I did not know that it is impossible to experience anger without feeling victimized, even on a subtle energy level. Though I did not understand this anger, I felt "done-to," which I eventually learned is a way to internalize victimization. Granted, this does not justify a wrong or harmful act. It does, however, imply the importance of moving through feelings of victimization. I learned that in order to have peace, resolve, and the enjoyment of living life grounded in the heart, one cannot remain in a victimized role. Forgiveness would be the ultimate goal in true resolution. And yes, sometimes this must involve forgiveness of self as well.

I was trying to resolve those feelings, and I joined an eight-week course called "Awakening," led by one of my earlier teachers, Jessica Dibb, a very devoted leader in the Baltimore spiritual community. The main intention of this course was to help participants clear and rebalance each of the chakras along with their corresponding emotional energies.

Remember that stuck emotional energy has to go somewhere, just like I shared in the "break-through" crystal story earlier. Looking at the trash can symbolically, I can now deduce that it represented the spiritual trash cans of unresolved stuff or "waste" that must be released in life. It is actually "wasted" if

we don't resolve and release it. When we release it, it trans-
forms as we integrate our lessons. Fires are about destruction,
rebirth, and renewal. The "trash" becomes ash as we release it
into the sacred teacher it needs to be! The following poem, "It
Could Be Tomorrow," which I wrote several years after the fire,
reflects the desire to release emotional pain into ash, but feeling
the call of more to learn for the soul lesson to be completed:

It could be tomorrow...

the sun could parch the perennial pain.
Grasping roots would open their certain gnarly hands.
Pain, parched, and baked-out dry,
would flake and crumble into
powder velvet ash.

I would carry it in an urn...
this sacred teacher, pain.

It would be bottled and safe from exploding,
calming, velvet, powdered ash—at rest and meditating.
The stilled ash would beckon
my ear to the urn.
I'd hear echoes of
what could still be received and learned...

There is more to this painful story that Grace infused into
my life; that of graces that came in the moments as the event
occurred. These are the smaller "graces" that our Sister Grace
brings to temper our pain as we recover. Even though Grace
spares no expense on our soul lessons, she provides kindnesses
and relief along the way, not allowing us to hurt and suffer any
more than is needed as we learn what must be learned.

There were many saving graces as I moved through the pain
of this loss in my life. With saving graces, Sister Grace always

brings the important lesson of how very much we are loved.

There was the kindness of strangers and acquaintances, people who I did not know personally. My neighbors, with their loving energy, constantly checked on me and expressed compassion. I felt such gratitude in my heart for their kindness; it helped me to smile through tears and pain.

The staff at the hotel where I lived for two months, while my home was being renovated, exuded great kindness in the midst of my pain and recovery. My physical comforts were met very well, and their kindness also helped me smile through my grief. There was even grace from the insurance company who covered the majority of the loss for a small deductible. They not only made the process easy, but also put me in a hotel that fed me breakfast every day, and would give me a ride if I needed it within a ten-mile radius.

I also must acknowledge the heartfelt kindness of the blessed firemen who did not have to save even one cat (my neighbors told me that they gave my surviving cat resuscitation and rushed her to the animal hospital with lights and siren). I felt tremendous gratitude toward them for saving the life of my little four-year-old, Oreo, and allowing us to share the journey of recovery.

Oreo and Tux made the ultimate sacrifice out of love. Tux died, and Oreo suffered for a year in order to be a part of the birthing of the soul lesson from the fire that I may now bring to others. Tux died for the lessons of Sister Grace, and Oreo recovered with the help of Sister Grace.

From my colleagues at work, I received the most heartfelt support and understanding. To my friends who never judged me, I offer gratitude for helping me through my cries of self-blame so patiently and lovingly.

And I am grateful to my family, who never once judged me or assigned blame. They allowed me to cry and cry as they kept telling me with undying patience that it was not my fault. They loved me unconditionally through this as they would have in anything, with no exceptions. I pray I have been able to provide the same for them, because I feel such deep gratitude in my heart. And, as a saving grace to myself, I kept functioning and participating in my life and my obligations.

Another type of saving grace that Grace brings is the type where we get spared from what does not need to happen in order to learn our lessons of the soul. I have deep gratitude to Grace that no people died and that one of my two cats lived.

What a beautiful thing it was to see Oreo reach out for life. At first, she risked death as she lay in a fully enclosed oxygen tank for two days, unable to breathe on her own. The veterinarians told me that she may need to be put to sleep or that there was a good chance she would survive disabled and unable to walk again. I was so scared and overwhelmed by the responsibility to choose for my sweet Oreo as I received that news.

I went to my spiritual teacher at that time and asked her what to do. She told me to reach inside, to find and give love, and to ask Oreo with my heart what she wanted me to do. I had never done anything like that before. I was not very familiar with connecting that way for it required being in touch with my heart and not my fear.   Nonetheless, I went to visit her the next day as I did everyday at the veterinary hospital. I asked her with my heart, "Oreo, do you want to live? Please, show me what I should do."

She had no muscle control for those first several days and could not even lift her head an inch before that moment. All of a sudden, she lifted her head and meowed a very clear meow. My heart cried tears of hope as I took that to be a sign that she wanted to live, and I promised her I would do everything possible to support her in her choice.

After a month, Oreo came to live with me at the hotel, where she continued her recovery with holistic medicine. Through the aid of acupuncture, herbal remedies, Reiki (a form of energy healing), and a wellspring of love, I watched this darling reach for life with all her heart and all her soul.

I got to know her cries like a mother with a baby. I knew when she had to relieve herself and made a special litter box area for her so that, when she was eventually able to walk, there was easy access. At first I had to hold her while she relieved herself because she had no muscle control and could not walk. I watched her take her first step and fall over, then take one and stand, then two, three, four.... and then she actually tried to jump onto the bed and fell off! I was shocked and in love with her. "I can't," had never entered her meow vocabulary. Then she leaped and made it onto the bed! One of the graces that came through my connection to Oreo and her healing journey was a lesson in learning to connect more in the heart as part of my own healing journey.

A little while later, about six months after Oreo and I had moved back home, we acquired "Grace," the cat. Grace was the only cat I had ever brought into my life that I named before I got her. I went out looking for "Grace" for me and Oreo to honor all that Sister Grace had brought, in the lessons, the comfort, and the sparing. Grace (the cat) came home and Oreo approved.

During that first year at home, Oreo nearly made a full recovery. All that remained was a little involuntary shaking of her head when she would eat her food. Other than that, she resumed her life as a fully functional cat for five more years. She died at the age of nine of a sudden onset of asthma. I do not know whether the fire shortened her life of not. What I do know is that she, like Tux, sacrificed in the highest and most divine way for the lessons of my life to be delivered. What brave and unconditionally loving souls they both were.

Because of this event in my life, I can now share with you, my readers, from a much deeper place, how important it is that we quench the fires of fear from the small scared self. As we lovingly take the hand of our small scared self, we can lead her into our hearts for healing! I could have only written this story and known its lessons after I had released self-blame. And, remember that self-blame comes from the small self because we have to make ourselves unworthy in order to feel that we are even deserving of blame. You can see that this is not the way to go. We would only be in a vicious cycle then, like the dog chasing its tail.

A most significant soul lesson I learned from the fire is how to deal with trauma. The trauma of the fire in my life taught me how to deal with and release repressed trauma from my childhood. All the lessons for dealing with trauma were in this

painful experience:
- releasing self-blame
- moving into self-acceptance
- the necessity of self-forgiveness
- reaching out to loved ones for support
- letting the love in
- accepting the ways in which we get spared where the trauma could have been greater, and
- connecting in the heart in order to release fear

Certainly, in any painful, emotional trauma, these points can serve to guide us to resolution and peace. This is the ultimate lesson of the fire and the most important sharing I can bring to you in resolving your life traumas.

It is my utmost prayer that these words will reach the hearts of each and every one of you. The more of you my story reaches, the more Grace expands into your hearts as well. It can be like a candle that lights your candle and we can share in what would then be the healing flame.

∞∞∞∞∞∞∞∞∞∞∞∞∞∞∞∞∞

There is another layer to this story to be shared, that of synchronicities, another way to connect with the divine magic of our world. Synchronicities are meaningful coincidences that most often come at a time of major soul lessons. They are energy attracting like energy and are usually amplified at stronger rites of passage throughout life. We can call them mile markers that indicate we are aligned with our path.

What follows are examples of synchronicities that showed up during my time of recovery from the fire—the first time I became aware of them. Synchronicities have become a comfort to me; they have helped to remind me that there is a divine order from which we are all a part and from which we are all in sync.

When I look back, I can see why I became aware of them during one of the first major soul lessons in my life, one that has taken me more than twenty years to complete. Synchronicities are often Sister Grace's way of saying, "Hey, we've got a big one coming," or "We are moving through a big one here, and we aren't done yet, so buckle up for the ride."

The most compelling synchronicity for me during recovery from the fire happened when I was buying replacement items for my home at Bed Bath and Beyond. Oreo had just moved to the hotel with me and I still did not know how complete her recovery would be. While standing in the checkout line, I noticed a calendar for the coming year, which was a month away, on the rack at the checkout. I half-absently picked it up as I noticed it to be a calendar of cats.

To my shock, on the very first page, the January cat was an exact duplicate of my Oreo to the placement and shape of every black spot on white fur. The calendar duplicate of Oreo was reaching up in vitality to the top of a vase where there was a healthy yellow rose blossoming.

I was awestruck at this amazing example; I knew with my heart that this represented her return to vitality. Sure enough, she ended up reaching the fullness of her recovered vitality that first year.

Some other very powerful synchronistic occurrences happened as I moved through emotional trauma toward recovery. My dear friend, Dave, gave me a book, *The Artful Cat* (Running Press Book Publishers, 1991) by Mark Bryant. In my hotel room, I was flipping through it and came upon Tux's double to the exact markings, just as I had with the calendar Oreo. What really made this compelling to the point of my bursting into tears was the accompanying photo. This "Tux" cat was laying down in front of tombstones! Next to the photo, the last two lines of an anonymous poem read, "There breathes no kitten of thy line, but would have given his life for thine." Tux was only six months old when he died in the fire.

One week before I moved back to my condo, my parents came to visit me at the hotel. When they arrived, they spotted a white dove perched on my car. Only recently, I looked up the meaning of "dove" and learned that in Catholicism, the dove is symbolic of the Holy Spirit arriving from heaven. In the Old Testament, doves were believed to embody the souls of the dead. I realized that the dove may have been the soul of

Tux. Universally, the dove symbolizes peace and faith to quiet our worries and troubled thoughts. It has even been said that the dove is a gentle reminder that there is always hope and to appreciate the simple blessings that go unnoticed in the chaos.[19] Wow—this was like the saving graces of Sister Grace!

There were synchronicities related to the hotel where I stayed and to the coming date of my return home. The name of the hotel where I stayed was "Woodfin Suites." Amazing! Wood easily represented the fire and the fin represented fish (that relates to the aquarium, the literal and emotional "holding tank" where I received the news of the fire).

After Oreo died, there were astounding synchronicities that immediately preceded and followed her death. Three weeks before her death, a ladybug landed on my chest at two different times while I was in bed. I was on the phone with my spiritual teacher and asked her the meaning of the ladybug since two had visited me in a rather short duration of time. She immediately responded, "Ladybug, ladybug, fly away home. Your house is on fire and your kids are alone!" I was overcome with emotion as I flashed back to the fire and considered her life shortened possibly due to the trauma she endured five years earlier.

That same night, I was watching a late-night talk show and the host was interviewing an Olympic gold medalist who suffered from asthma. He asked, "What is it like to live with?" The medalist responded, "It's like having a cold and then sticking your head in mud and trying to breathe." This was emotionally overwhelming and hard for me to hear.

Only one day after she died, I was watching a movie where there was a scene at a veterinary practice. There was an IV bag hanging in the background. I had just taken down the one I had for Oreo's home treatment just before she died. Two days later, I was watching a TV sitcom and there was a veterinary scene yet again! On the commercial break that followed was a commercial for Oreo cookies that ended with "only Oreo." The very next commercial, I kid you not, was an ad for a movie, *A Time to Kill*. I was overcome with emotional pain. It punctuated my grief and despair.

All of these events in such a short period following her

death, as you can imagine, were deeply heart-wrenching for me. I concluded that these synchronicities reflected the deep love I had for Oreo, as well as the emotional memories of the trauma. Synchronicities often appear as amplifications of strong emotional energies we are experiencing.

On that note, there are two additional and deeply meaningful synchronicities related to the fire that occurred, believe it or not, within the last two hours, during the very writing of this chapter. The first one happened as I got to the part about the strong-smelling ashes. At the very moment of writing those words, I realized I had been carrying around in my pocket five small pieces of obsidian as grounding stones, not knowing in the morning when I put them there what I would be writing for you today. Obsidian is known to be a grounding stone that can help us stay in the heart and not move into fear.

As I was writing the words, I felt the need to pause and make contact with the obsidian pieces, triggered by a stirring of old emotions and inner compassion in memory of this story. I reached into my pocket to hold them. As I was holding them, I realized I was holding a rock born out of the strongest fire know to humankind, that of volcanoes! So, there I was reaching for the outcome of the strongest fire to ground me as I was telling the story of my condo fire. In introducing you to Sister Grace and her saving graces, she provided me the obsidian this morning that I would need for support as I would later share my story of the Fireside fire.

Another synchronicity related to the fire followed about an hour later. My writer's group broke for lunch right after I wrote the part about Oreo moving back to the hotel. I sat among my comrades, and Elaina was at my table. You may recall that she was my myofascial release practitioner from the day before, after I had lost 3,000 words of writing. Well, we were chatting and getting to know each other better, asking each other questions typical of when you first meet someone. I asked her how long she had lived in Sedona, and she said six months. She then told me that she moved from the Washington, D.C. area after falling in love with Sedona. I asked her where near D.C.—I had lived in the D.C. suburbs at one point. To be exact, I lived in Gaithersburg, Maryland, at the time of the fire. She spoke and said she had lived in Gaithersburg for twenty years and had moved here from there. I nearly shit a brick!

Okay, forgive me; I know that's not the most spiritual way to put it. But I was amazed at this synchronicity that had just come after writing this story for the first time in my life. Furthermore, I am writing of it twenty years after its occurrence, having moved back to my condo in January 1991, almost the exact amount of time that Elaina said she had lived in Gaithersburg. Then we met here in Sedona, and I practically fell into her arms in despair as she supported me through grief.

There is one more synchronicity that occurred during the final revision of this chapter, back home in Baltimore. During this last revision, I was in the middle of a major home repair of a busted water main pipe in my front yard. To the very hour that I had written the final revision of this Fireside fire chapter, the men were outside replacing the pipe. I had just paid the plumber. All of a sudden it hit me. This was the first time since the fire twenty years ago, that I had to file a homeowner claim. I had just put the claim check from my homeowner's policy in the bank the morning of this revision and paid the plumber right in the middle of the chapter.

The story begins with fire and ends with water. Amazing Grace!

Chapter Twenty

Discernment and Self-Care

The next story will broaden our understanding of synchronicities. The story includes lessons of discernment, more lessons on connecting in the heart, and learning not to push with the head and the small, fear-based self. It is important to learn to connect with the true discernment of our hearts—that which serves our higher good. If we discern from the head only, we risk the false, ego-attached interpretations of the small self. This is how we stay ahead of Coyote and his shape-shifter, ego self, who would gladly steal the moment.

When I was in my mid-thirties, I was about to embark on what I considered to be one of the greatest trips I would take in my life. I had discovered this trip from a group called Earthwatch Institute, a global environmental organization that was going to the Four Corners region of the United States. They needed artists to hike into the desert, including areas where no one was known to hike before. They were creating a quest to find undiscovered petroglyphs, sketch them, and catalogue these sketches.

I was so excited! I was always interested in archaeology, and I was an artist who enjoyed drawing. I carried with me a deeply adventurous spirit and a love for the feel of my feet on the earth in explorer mode. This has been one of the greatest essences of my spirit that I have enjoyed. This trip had my name on it, right? Right, except that I vehemently ignored one not so small eighty-five–pound detail: At that time in my life, I was about eighty-five pounds overweight, and my pioneering spirit was trapped inside this weight. My adventurous spirit had not carried this weight for most of my life and was in denial of its existence. For thirty-three of my then thirty-eight years of life, I had been weight proportionate and was used to being able to do things that required physical fitness. Reasons I did not understand at the time had triggered the change, but I still saw the world as a very high-energy person.

I had not fully come to grips with this bodily change. It was at most a barely conscious whisper that I kept kicking aside, not ready to hear that it was a cry. In no way did I want to recognize that I may not be fit for this amazing trip. If I had admitted that to myself at the time, I would then have been faced squarely with confronting the issues that were trapped inside my body. Coyote Trickster worked hard to not let me see this and encouraged me to see only the world from my face outward—rather than from my full reflection.

Intellectually, I knew I was overweight, but I pushed this truth away as much as I could. I wanted to take part in the passionate fun parts of life, and not in another lesson toward the work of the soul. Even though I so badly wanted this trip to be right for me, I was at least rationally aware that just maybe I was in over my head. On one level, I wanted to take care of myself and not put myself in harm's way, and on another level my confused ego shape-shifter was pushing with my head for the outcome I wanted. And guess what happened: the "perfect storm," complete with bugle calls from Grace!

Remember, Grace sends synchronicities at times of heightened intensity and when she feels that we are ready for a major soul lesson. It was the first time in five years of weight gain that a little nudge of reality crept in along with an inkling of concern.

Coyote Trickster did not like this, but the sheer physical demands of the trip nudged Coyote at least into a slight wobble.

The synchronicities poured in and were, as synchronicities often are, compelling, to say the least. I will share the strongest of them for you to connect with my experience.

As I moved through this decision that I considered extremely important in my life, the first synchronicity smacked me in the face. During the decision, I was pulling out of my street on the way to work and I saw a dog swaggering in the middle of the street; it looked like it was inflicted with mange. I started to pass the dog, and then my heart caught up to the moment. I thought this dog could get run over if I did not go back and try to help.

One block away was a veterinary office and I stopped in to ask them if they could help me out. They could not, but suggested that the police are usually willing to keep a dog for a day until arrangements could be made. With that, I got back into the car to get the dog. I went back to the spot, but he was nowhere to be found. I pulled over, figuring he must have wandered into the nearby backyards where I could not see him.

Off I went into someone's backyard and was immediately confronted with a six-foot metal sculpture of Kokopelli. Kokopelli is known as the Hopi Indian flute player and has been discovered many times in petroglyphs.

"Oh, baby, yeah," said my head severed from my heart. Little did I know, my true heart was not involved in this exclamation, as the emotion I felt made me deceptively sure I was connecting with my heart. I thought this must surely mean that I was meant to take this trip. I was ignorant of the fact that, among meanings of Kokopelli, he is known as the trickster and the healer. My slick little Coyote had enlisted a companion, and I didn't know it.

But what about the mangy dog? Coyote did not want me to consider at the time that the mangy dog was a powerful synchronicity, too. I just thought the dog had led me to the Kokopelli, but only literally. Boy, did I miss a big one! If I had taken that trip, I would have been like that mangy dog, swaggering and staggering, desperately in need of help as I labored all 217 pounds of me miles and miles through the desert to the petroglyphs.

Grace gives us the choice, and we decide to get it or she

will lovingly continue to pave the road of our soul lesson du jour. Herein resides the importance of discernment. We must be careful with the definitions we assign to synchronicities as we notice them in our lives. The desires of the small self may not reflect our true needs. We must not assign our preferred meanings to synchronicities, but direct them to speak through our hearts and not our heads for the true meaning.

The more we are grounded in love in the heart and come from this divine energy, the more we are able to correctly discern for ourselves in the moment. On another note, there is never a wrong choice, only a choice to get the lesson we need sooner or later. I could not find the mangy dog, the dog I would not *see*.

From a heart level, the mangy dog was a sign not to go, and a sign to take care of the obesity issues that were interfering with what my natural vitality wanted to do. Even though the coordinator from Earthwatch warned me that we would be hiking nine miles a day, my desire blinded my needs. I retorted that I had gotten a physical and that the doctor said I was physically healthy enough to go (surprising, but he did).

So, mangy-dog-blinded, I lay in bed doing a crossword puzzle that night and another synchronicity arrived with the puzzle. One of the clues was "encampment" and the answer was "bivoac," which was exactly what we would be setting up as we hiked our way through the desert. Well, I was about to get my "just dessert." The crossword clue easily coaxed my blinded desire.

Excitedly, I contacted the coordinator the next day and signed up. I bought a tremendous amount of camping gear in preparation, as well as my plane ticket, and paid Earthwatch. Four days before the trip, with gear all over my living room floor, I received a very distressed call from the archaeologist who was already out in the field and had to call me by radio phone. It quickly became clear that she did not want me to join their excursion. She was very distressed that she wasn't contacted by Earthwatch first and that, in her opinion, I was too overweight to handle the trip. I convinced myself that I had just gotten tangled in negative energy that wasn't about me but must have been about the archaeologist and the Earthwatch coordinator.

Remember, my reader friends, in spiritual matters it is always about you and your responsibility to everything you create in your life; you create all of your life events. I was missing this point. Sister Grace is always orchestrating. Wherever you go, there you are! I didn't know this yet.

I was sure that the archaeologist just did not know Caren Appel! In this manner, she knew me better than I knew myself, and told me that if I could not keep up with the group they would leave me behind. If that happened, she explained that I would have to be helicoptered out of there at my expense. I was indignant and very distressed, but I realized there was no way I could take this trip because I felt unsupported. I didn't know, of course, how very supportive this was of her both for me and for the good of the team. I thank her now in my heart for her integrity.

So Grace had brought me a giant wake-up call for healing my body and the emotional issues that were stored in my obesity. At the time, I didn't get it simply because I was not ready. Instead, I felt as if my world had fallen apart and went into almost a spiritual crisis. Having misinterpreted the synchronicities, I felt betrayed by God and did not recognize my own self-betrayal. Coyote won that round of hide-and-go-seek, but not the final round regarding my obesity lesson, as you will see. I lost my spiritual faith for a little while, not understanding and knowing Sister Grace at that time.

Chapter Twenty-One

Releasing Anger into Love

It is time to share more clearly with you how I gained and retained the weight. I was thirty years old, about three years past the fire, and feeling very depressed and sad. I had continued to feel that some type of trauma had happened to me in my life that I couldn't quite remember. I had flashes of abuse that didn't make sense to me. It was not parental, but it seemed to center around two key people. I was angry and felt victimized, but I couldn't put a finger on the picture clearly. I had difficulty functioning at work and knew I had to do something.

I was very holistically oriented and preferred a natural approach for treating depression, but I did not understand well enough such approaches and the appropriate options. I decided to go on an anti-depressant for the first time in my life. Within nine months of starting the anti-depressant, I gained thirty pounds and, within a total of a year and three months, I had effortlessly amassed a total of sixty-pounds. The medication had clearly triggered it, but it was actually anger and its toxic energy that allowed me to carry that weight for nearly ten years and amass an additional twenty-plus pounds beyond that.

In my early thirties, I thought I had the answer for everyone and I was sure that I was only trying to help. I was *always* just trying to help. But I didn't realize that I was not responsible for their *clarity*, only mine. I was sure that if, by my definition, someone had done me wrong, it was my job to tell them and it was their job to fix it.

Can you relate? Have you ever been riddled with what I now realize was righteous indignation? We can be completely right about someone else, how they've acted out on others, and what they need to do or what would help them, and it still does not matter. They need to learn from Sister Grace in their own divine timing. I did not realize that in any situation when you try to make someone conform to your definition and to your timing, you are playing a game of a false, addicted god over their world.

I learned several years later that any human being has a totally human right to act in whatever way they choose, even in a perfectly screwed-up way. As I said earlier, no matter how bad the behavior of the other person is, they are not trying to offend you. They are only acting out of their own drama. "Smile, you're on *Candid Camera!*" That's right! Do you see it now? I'll bet it's getting clearer! Their stuff is actually not about you and it is not your concern.

Remember, we do have the right to draw boundaries, but the way we heal others is by the return to compassion and love for ourselves, and then for each other, as we send healing waves out into the world. I know the hardest thing to do is to wish healing for the person who has hurt you. This does not mean you need to be in relationship with the person at all. We established earlier that in some cases it could be very toxic to do so and may not be safe at all to engage with that person in any way.

Now, in some cases yes, it can be an extremely powerful healing to confront the person who has hurt you. Be careful, though, because your purpose would not be to make them understand, but to make the space for your own feelings to count. It's possible you may never speak to them again after that. Or, if they are ready, very powerful healing can happen for the both of you.

I am a therapist who believes it is not essential to forgive others, at least initially, in every situation. Forgive then, only yourself and, your inability to forgive the other. Due to the magnitude of the trauma, you may not be able to get that far. But that's okay! Love yourself and accept how far you can go. You may even hold some anger that you feel you are not willing to let go of. I lovingly tell you that while that may not be the highest ideal, sometimes we need the emotional protection of anger until we have strengthened ourselves further. Please honor yourself and please be gentle with yourself.

I will say, however, in all cases without fail, that it is very necessary to wish them healing in your heart. Start with that, please. In some cases it will lead you to forgive them. At the very least it will lead you to a softening of your heart—this I guarantee. It will help you in your journey of letting go and returning to your own beautiful, divine, clear, full spectrum of fluid light. This is the path home to your heart. Even if you can't let go all the way, it will at least help you soften your anger so that you will not be sending out ripples that are harmful to you and onward through the layers of life.

As long as you stay rooted in anger, you are still acting out of fear and your small self. I love you enough to tell you this, even though this may be extremely difficult for you to hear. Then, when you are ready and able to reach forgiveness in your heart, you will be sending out the most amazing ripples, the kind that completely heal the heart. These are the kind that heal the world.

Please know, dear friends, that in no way am I discounting your feelings or meaning to push you in any way. My strong and direct way of saying this is only to help you release the chains that bind you. These are the chains of emotional expectation that say, "I need you to be this way for me to feel fine in the world," and the chains that keep you in anger when others don't step up to the plate. With deep compassion and love for you, I pray that any painful experiences you have had will only lead you back to your own heart and out of the fear of the small self. Please take her hand—that hurt and scared part of you! She needs your compassion and for you to bring her into your heart for healing. I stayed fat in the need to learn that lesson.

My anger remained cushioned in my obese body to ab-sorb the shocks along the way. There it felt safe and secure. I didn't realize I was directing anger ultimately to myself. What Grace presented for me was that I had to return to self-love and become much more grounded in the heart or I would not be able to release the weight effectively. I remember the first day I peeked around the tree during hide-and-go-seek and caught the shadow clearly, if only for a moment. It was four years after the mangy-dog-Earthwatch lesson. This next lesson in re-turning to self-love was joined in continued lessons of discern-ment, connecting in the heart, and not pushing with our heads and the small, ego-driven self.

I was closer to becoming ready for this lesson of self-love and grounding in the heart. During that trip, denial began to crack open. I finally allowed myself to know that I would have to face my fears and master self-love if I was to heal this body where my pioneering spirit had been trapped.

This time I went on a five-day sea kayaking trip, off the coast of Washington state, desperate for my body to just behave so I could have my adventures. No anger there, hah! I sure wasn't lazy, but I was afraid to face myself and didn't know it. As a result, I was unkind to my body—and, in that sense, myself. I didn't know I was taking my unexpressed anger out on my body, which was doing the best it could to house my pent-up anger from many years of feeling the world needed to change so that I could be just fine.

The trip took place in the San Juan Islands nestled among Mt. Baker, Mt. Rainier, and the Canadian Rockies. We planned to kayak twenty miles in five days and camp out on the islands. Orca whale watching was a highlighted feature.

When I learned of the trip, I was ecstatic. I had not been this excited since the Earthwatch trip. A couple of details gnawed at my consciousness just a tad: one, I had never been sea kayak-ing, a minor detail in my pioneering brain. (This is the same pioneering brain that once tried to paint an entire level of my house in one weekend!) And, of course, nudging at the edge of my consciousness was the fact that I was still eighty-five or so pounds overweight and living life in my protected cocoon.

Was it time to give birth to the butterfly yet? I didn't even know there was a need. Coyote Trickster and his misconstrued ego quickly grabbed up the reins of my pioneering spirit and yanked me away from self-care and rationality. I was at least honest about my weight with the trip leaders when I called to inquire but insisted that my tenacity would make up for any lack of strength. They assured me that prior experience was not required, and they seemed convinced by my determination that I could handle it.

So off I went on the trip, paired in a double kayak with "Ms. New York." I can't remember her name, and I am lovingly referring to her as "Ms. New York" because of my enjoyment of her New York accent and accompanying vitality. Day one of the trip began, and I wasn't holding my own. We were falling behind the rest of the group, and I felt embarrassed and ashamed. At one point, I was fluctuating between imagining being helicoptered out of this rip-tide nightmare and then yelling "fuck" really loud on each stroke of the paddle, trying to get my strength and energy up for the quagmire I had gotten myself into. So I was yelling, "Fuck, fuck...fuckkk,'" and "Ms. New York," who was very good-natured and sweet kept saying to me, "That's right, Caren, just yell 'fuckkk.'" Somehow, I got through the first day and I was amazed that "Ms. New York" and I arrived not too far behind everyone else.

On a separate note, an orca whale pod came in very close to us that day. The experience was blissful. At least eight of them surrounded our kayaks and came up breaching. We could hear their breaths through their blowholes as they showcased their perfect spirits and bodies.

Later that night at our encampment (yes, I finally got my encampment experience), one of the trip guides, Patricia, came over to me and said, "Oh, Caren, I forgot to tell you that you are sitting too low in the kayak. You are too short and you are not making a good cut-in with the water as a result. So, tomorrow we will raise you up with your air mattress and you will be fine." "Oh, joy of joy of joy," I thought, as I happily concluded that I was wrong after all. I smugly surmised to myself, "I'm not too fat to handle this trip after all; thank you very much." If I were a whale, I was sure I could swim and breach with grace. So, the next day, followed by Coyote and his inflated ego, I pumped myself up and Patricia pumped me up with the air mattress. I was not only fine, but no kidding, "Ms. New York" and I were passing everyone else and keeping up with the guides!

While the air mattress and Coyote Trickster had inflated me, I hadn't realized that the next day I was about to be painfully deflated. Apparently, I had good upper-body strength despite my obesity, but my lower body strength was severely compromised. That next day, we gave our upper bodies a break from kayaking and went on a hike. Within the first half-mile, I fell severely behind the group. I wasn't even able to see them anymore, and finally I sat down by a tree and cried and cried. Breakthrough! I was terrified and despairing.

So, what happened next? What came with the breakthrough was the physical recognition of my weight problem. But that was not enough. I was missing the connection to anger and the need to return to love, the most important part of all. I hated my body now that I finally allowed myself to see it. I felt low, ashamed, and embarrassed that I had allowed myself to get so out of hand. After the trip I didn't lose the weight; instead, I began to hide.

During the year that followed, I went to a conference in southern Utah and stayed at a campground that had a wonderful hot spring pool right on the grounds. I wanted to get in the pool so badly, but I hadn't allowed myself to wear a bathing suit for ten years. I had felt so ashamed of myself. I slipped into the pool when I thought no one saw me and slipped out only when I thought the coast was clear. I didn't want to disgust anyone with my body. The water felt so good, I could almost cry! A friend I made on the trip saw my attempts to slip privately in and out. She picked up on my discomfort and offered some very loving words to me about accepting myself and loving myself in order to heal. My heart was beginning to thaw.

A little later that year I was visiting a cousin in California, and I went to a great spa resort with mineral pools and mud baths. I couldn't take the self-abuse anymore, and the pain of letting go became a lot less than the pain of holding on, like the addict who becomes sick and tired of becoming sick and tired. I decided I was just as worthy as anyone else and that I had the right to enjoy the water, too! Finally, I allowed myself freedom through the first beginnings of nurturing and loving my body and releasing shame. Something was happening—a peaceful calm, a kind nudging of self-acceptance. The small self in my big body was letting go of anger. I began to feel worthy to take that thirteen-inch journey back to my heart where I could finally nurture my hurt and scared self who had tried to rule the show for so very long. A poem I wrote a short time prior to this moment entitled, "My Dawn," reflects this reawakening:

She came to me, bright and peaceful,
and lifted the once stuck shade in my room...
my room, so full of space and opening
with Dawn...

Now Dawn...
And I am awakening, fully alive.
She nurtured me in her arms,
and I rose free—
my Dawn,
me.

I will always value that day at the hot springs where I liberated my imprisoned spirit as I began to reclaim my worthiness. I pranced around in my bathing suit unabashed with no need to even cover up with a towel, and soaked in the clear crystalline waters of the mineral pools and of my true spirit! Grace and Clarity smiled.

Having lost the weight of fear, I faced the fear of weight. I basked and bathed under nurturing pillow clouds and life-augmenting sun. On that day, I also went into the mud bath and slathered my loving body with cleansing mineral clay. I felt as if I could hear my body cry out in relief and joy as I allowed it to relax and be soothed in the sun that was forming in my heart on this beautiful and vibrant day.

I wrote the following poem, "Love Kept Faith," in the middle of my anger/weight crisis in 1998 but revised it many years later after I had transformed my anger-body into a healed state:

The deep, brown, soppy, caked mud creaked and groaned
from an old, settled state of false victory.
It had rained at times then and now, so moisture
pinned itself under a dry, brownie-glazed shell.
The soft inside cradled its captor captive and breathing.

Narrow tension lines, uncertain at first and almost sluggish,
split slowly the brownie shell...
A fleshy pink pale pointer ground dirt in its nail
as it gripped the crumbling giving casement—
and then took in air as if it alone could breathe.

Navigating the shell, once thought fierce,
the blind pink periscope pointer rose and fell,
rose and fell like a solo building wrecker
and crumbled the old, settled shell...

Pinhole light brought mockery or hope
depending on thought alone.
And thought depended on its-elf alone,
a riddle from Grace, and she was laughing in love.

Love kept faith protecting thought in divine, knowing light.
The fleshy periscope pointer stepped up vigor and might,
unveiling a flexing mass of pink pale pointers adjoined.
With love and will they scraped and dug,

scraped and dug, and dug deep and wide,
their steam shovel arms emerging to join
the volitional dance,
now pounding, swinging, exuberantly commanding,
yet surrendered in a meditation of moving mountains...

The temple of her body was wholly birthed.
Exposed and relieved, she basked and bathed
under nurturing pillow clouds and life-augmenting sun.

For so many years, my small self had been protecting me from what I thought was a mean world. As long as I carried anger, and even though I worked very hard not to project it, the vibrational energy of it still lived within me. This negative vibration had to go somewhere. Mostly, I turned it inward, and it became fuel to sustain my obesity. I also turned it into the gambling addiction I wrote of earlier.

For a while I thought I hated men because they didn't want to date me anymore, not realizing the negative vibration I was sending out. I hated the world at large from their many cruel jokes about obese people. I couldn't even go to a movie without receiving an assault from an actor's line.

Yes, the assaults were real, but I wasn't in a state of self-love. Had I been in a state of self-love, it is much more likely that I would have attracted a man who resonated to be with me rather than the men who never asked for a second date. In no way was I an angry bitch on these dates. I was actually a very positive, fun-loving person who could laugh and have great conversation. The ripples we send out do not have to be verbal at all; rather, it is the energy we carry that the world responds to, and much of this is unconscious. In the positive, this is illustrated by the Maharishi Effect, as the masses respond unconsciously to the loving energy of the transcendental meditation.

It is so very important that we love this scared part who is only trying to protect us. This cannot be overstated. When we bring this hurt, oil-stained self into the refinery of the heart for healing, we can then truly arrive back home to our God-connected, divine selves. And we learn that this is the home we have been looking for, the one where we are our own divine housekeepers. What do you think finally happened next? Well, I went to a gym, and showed up in flowered shorts more fit for gardening. Flower power! In the garden of my divine self, I was about to clear the weeds and nurture my God-given seeds. I hadn't been to a gym since I played racquetball twelve years earlier. I was a little afraid that I wouldn't fit in, but mostly I realized that it was my choice whether to fit in, and that I create my own reality. My choice! I walked in, announced myself, and stated that I had an appointment with a trainer.

Over the next eleven months I shed ninety-one pounds through healthy nutrition, exercise and, most of all, self-love! In this newly discovered state of self-love for my body, I hired a trainer at first so that I would not feel so overwhelmed. Then I continued solo and at times with workout friends, walking out of the ninety-one pounds by loving myself and my body every step of the way.

Are you feeling how devastating it can be to live through the addicted small self in fear? The addicted self wants to make everyone else responsible for change. This addicted small self would rather harbor anger, fueled with the heavy-leaded belief that the world is a screwed-up place with screwed-up people in it, than be open to true love, which is grounded in the heart. It is in the heart where we take responsibility for our own ripples, our true place in the world. Are you feeling it more and more? This is the only way that we heal the world and ourselves.

I honor the path of wellness in my body, with all of its successes and challenges to teach me along the way. I want you to understand a most significant part: I could not have learned to honor my newly transformed body until I learned to love myself in my body when it was in its obesity. This is a deep lesson in self-love. The day at the hot springs, when I liberated my imprisoned spirit, was the day when I took my own hand.

Even if I did not fully understand it at the time, there was a dawning in me where I started to understand and accept that my loving body on some level was protecting me, shielding me in some way. I came to understand that it was my way of pushing away at the world where I had carried anger. In a way, my body was protecting me from further hurt. By learning to love my obese body and release my attachment to shame, I was ultimately able to heal my body by loving it through its changes.

You can see by my story, the oil-stained small self, in its hurt, is also a very loving soldier just trying to rescue and protect us from harm, albeit from a place of fear. This is why it is so important to bring those hurt parts of ourselves into the heart for refining in love. We cannot hate those parts of ourselves and simultaneously expect to heal them.

Think about it: if you have a child and you express anger and harsh judgment toward that child while trying to help him or her, will that child be more likely to thrive and change, or will he or she emotionally wither and break under the weight of your bearings? We must love the parts of ourselves that need healing for those parts to trust us and take our hand. Do you hold your hand out to yourself or do you push yourself away?

A few years later, I was bored with my fitness routine and gained some of the weight back. I joined fitness "boot camp," because I learned that I loved working out my body with other people, as it provided a social as well as supportive aspect for me. Plus, I came to value greatly the synergy of motivational group energy to propel my personal efforts and outcomes. As a result of boot camp, I have now become a seasoned runner, completed several races, and maintain a regular and consistent fitness routine.

My current trainer, Hugo Eraso, is an amazing man who has helped me learn more about self-honoring than I could have ever imagined would come from fitness boot camp. Hugo takes us to extreme levels of challenge with our bodies. He also models how to honor and love our bodies and ourselves. He is a man who exemplifies self-honor and inner commitment in all areas of life. He essentially teaches perseverance through self-love, and it shows in his following.

On any given Thursday morning at 5:30 a.m., about thirty of us show up for fitness training with him. We also devote every

Saturday and Sunday, showing up at 6:30 a.m., to do the same. Many of us work out additional days with him. I have learned that the average amount of time any one person has trained with him is easily a couple of years. So many stay! Very few leave his program. Several have been with him since he began at Bally Total Fitness over seven years ago.

What force could he possibly possess that causes so many to stay with him for so long? What force could get that many people out of bed on such a consistent basis, even in the summer rain and freezing days of winter? I know you've got it! Only self-love and self-honoring could produce such an effect. Love and honor yourself into your full wellness! The degree of ease toward positive change is correlated to the degree of self-love.

Think about it, if you have a weak moment in the process and you are filled with self-love, then you would not stop your energy flow with self-doubt. Energy cannot flow from the small self. Energy flows only from a loving state. Our small selves steal energy and our true loving selves are infinite in our energy because we are connected to God's infinite love. So move your personal mountain; you have the divine tool. It was always there and will never blame you, but will only uphold you.

Grace had provided me an interesting synchronicity that relates to the two types of settings in which I have spent the most of my earned money, one destructively and one in self-loving support. That is, I do my fitness routine at Bally Total Fitness, and I am, as you know, a recovering gambling addict. The same Bally has also owned casinos and manufactured slot machines. How do you invest yourself in your life?

To my readers who have brought the challenge of obesity into their lives, I compassionately and lovingly say to you that my story is not intended to be an explanation for every person that carries obesity in their lives. This challenge can be a very complicated journey with different layers and contributing factors. As you address this issue in your life, however, I promise you it will not feel nearly as overwhelming if you start this journey with love and compassion toward yourself in your obesity.

Anything we want to change in ourselves depends on self-love and self-compassion. If we hate the things we want to change, we are coming from the false, scared self again and cannot expect resolution to come from a place that is not real. In other words, the only real authentic you is the divine, God-connected you.

Remember that the small self is based on inventions of fear from the ego. Ego creates the personality defenses we form to protect ourselves from the hurts of the world. It is not of God. It is of an "oil rig," rigged by the oil spills from others when they were not aligned with God. So, if we try to heal from that point of view, we are trying to heal from something that is not real. It has nothing to do with the God-giving you.

Connect with your heart and love, love, love yourself all the way through your desired changes and you will be harnessing the transformative power of love. Think of a reverse ripple. The ripples we send out are in response to the world around us. In reverse, the ripples we create inwardly are our responses to ourselves.

Do you choose to respond with a reverse ripple of self-deprecation and self-loathing or a reverse ripple of self-love? Which one would allow you to achieve the changes you seek in yourself? We cannot hate the things we want to change and effectively change them. We cannot heal from a standpoint of self-hatred, but only from love.

Chapter Twenty-Two

Manifestation: The Reverse Ripple

M anifestation means the ability to consciously co-create with intention that which we want to bring into our lives. It is, in fact, a reverse ripple. So far, we understand the ripples that we send out into the world—their ever-expanding impact—and how they are affected by the quality of the relationship we have with ourselves. This aspect of the ripple effect is how we affect the world around us beginning with ourselves. Manifestation is the outcome of the ripples we send out, with our chosen thoughts and attitudes, as it creates an internal effect on the world within us. Manifestation then serves as a reverse ripple, as what comes back to us in a loop is based on what we put out.

The infinity symbol depicts this. It is a sideways figure eight. Imagine tracing the line of this sideways eight starting at the center point with the phrase, "All that I give I give to myself." When we consciously co-create our lives with intention, we choose the desire we wish to send out for the divine universe to receive like a radio tower and transmit back to us. It is driven by synchronistic energy, because in effect it is energy attracting like-energy. We become what we think. That is manifestation. It is the manner by which we send out a conscious signal for that which we wish to attract. The universe will reflect this perfectly back to us. Don't miss the power of this statement.

To the exact degree that you believe something will be true is the exact degree to which it will be true for you. If I was 90 percent sure I would reach my weight loss goal, then there was a 90 percent chance this would happen. If I was 40 percent sure, then I would have been putting a 40 percent chance out into the universe. Divine universal consciousness can only reflect back to you exactly what you reflect out. You *are* universal consciousness. How could you escape yourself and expect other than what is you? Do you see how amazingly powerful you really are?

We truly create our world and every aspect of it one thought at a time. This is in regard to any aspect of what we desire, a successful career, a marriage or life partner, financial abundance, a healthy body, the removal of an uncomfortable state like anxiety or depression, resolution of an issue, or the power to quit a bad habit. It must always involve a synergy between the mind and the heart; it cannot be devoid of the heart or the results would either not last or be at risk.

Any life outcome is vulnerable and not secure if it is not anchored with love in your heart. If a wish only comes from your head, it would be empty; it would come from some aspect of your disconnected self. Your emotions represent the heart aspect of your desires that serve as a carrier of the message. The universe can only respond to that which is essential, which would have to be grounded in the heart.

Many years ago, when the notion of conscious and intentional manifestation was new to me, I learned about research that had been done regarding dreams and our emotional states.[20] The researchers indicated that when a person had an emotional experience in the dream state, the brain could not tell the difference between real and imagined. Emotional feelings such as happiness, sadness, joy, despair, and love evoked the same chemical changes in the brain as if the individual was really experiencing those states. So, of course, they really were. But what was compelling about this to me was this implied that the brain cannot tell the difference between actual and imagined.

Think about it—have you ever awakened after a dream feeling like it had really happened? It is this consideration that I believe explains the magic of manifestation. Our brains respond to the emotions behind our thoughts the same way whether the thoughts involve actual or imagined events.

It's easy to conclude, therefore, that if we think it, and feel the emotional state connected to it, we create it. The point here is that manifestation cannot happen without the involvement of the heart and our emotions, just as I explained earlier in my interpretation of the Hundredth Monkey Phenomenon. When our emotions are involved, as the dream research illustrated, the brain cannot tell the difference between real and imagined. It is my interpretation of many of the popular manifestation books on the market, that authors often jump right in on a point that implies, "If you think it, you create it."

A much more accurate way of explaining manifestation is, "If you feel it, you create it." Anything you feel relates to either something you fear or something you want to love in yourself and others. So, the results of manifestation are directly driven by the ripples we send out—its engine, our emotions. As the reverse ripple, manifestation is how what we put out into the world comes back to us.

It can be driven by the small, scared self or the true, divine, loving self. In other words, if you project into the world a fear that you can't have or change something that personally matters, you are cementing that limitation right into your life. You have sent out an energy based on lack and powerlessness so that is what will be returned to you. Divine love only wants to show you who you are by what you reflect; it wants to make you responsible for who you are by reflecting you back to yourself. It cannot give you a beautiful and fit body while you hate it and feel disempowered. Manifestation is divine love showing you your chosen relationship to yourself!

This is certainly not because love is mean, it is because love wants you to reach for your highest self, for itself. If you put out a feeling of deprivation, it will reflect deprivation back to you; if you put out a feeling of "I can, I make happen, I will, I create, I bring to myself that which I truly desire," than so it shall be, because that is what love returns. Love returns *you* to *you*, in its divine mirror of truth, for you to uphold and resolve.

I have learned more about manifestation from fitness boot camp than I could have ever imagined, just as I have from its lessons of self-love. Hugo has become a powerful manifestation teacher in my life; he has beckoned me to go deeper within to achieve the results I currently enjoy. I have shared with you how love of ourselves is a part of the success of every person there. That is the heart aspect, what we then gear our minds toward manifesting makes the difference in our outcomes over and over without fail. Remember, manifestation responds both to the small self in fear and the heart-grounded self in love.

Before I joined fitness boot camp, I was not a runner. The first day, I could barely reach a quarter-mile without turning my stride to a walk. Two months later, I ran my first 5K race. Within the same time period, I ran eight to ten miles at one time during some of our weekend runs. When running a hill, I had the choice to say either, "This is too much; I can't do this" or "My body knows what to do and I'm going to make it to the next landmark." Connect your heart's desire with the thoughts you choose to transmit to run the hills of your life.

Again, we go deeper in our understanding of the essential importance of grounding ourselves through love in the heart. The divine source loves us so much that it wants us to realize that every possible outcome we desire already exists in the world of potentiality. What does that mean? It means because we are all connected as one to this loving, divine, one-source energy, all knowledge and outcomes are available to each and every one of us. When we "tap in" by imagining with our minds the outcomes we desire, and then feel them with the heart as if they already exist in our lives, we ultimately create them. This is the synergy of mind and emotion that creates the world we choose. Remember, if you want to know what your thoughts and feelings are doing, just look at the world around you. Choose consciously and, with loving intention, create the life you desire.

Chapter Twenty-Three

Resolving the Feedback Loop of The Reverse Ripple

Throughout this book, we have been exploring what happens when we send out negative ripples. How do they truly impact our lives? Earlier, I explained the difference in the directional momentum of our love-infused ripples versus our fear-based ripples. You may recall, a love-infused ripple is in harmony with God and is in alignment with our true self. In its completeness, it joins with God in infinity. A ripple infused with negative energy is laden with oil spills, so God lovingly returns them to us in a feedback loop to clean up for eventual transformation.

In the negative, we or others around us are operating out of original core wound energy, born out of the first oil spills we received. To resolve the negative ripple effect, we must be able to shield ourselves from the negative ripples of others so we don't take them on as our own. We must also be able to identify and transform our own negative ripples and not project our original core wounds through them.

The world is full of the vibration of negative ripples. To that end, you can be going about the day minding your own business and someone suddenly sends a negative ripple your way. I call it "psychological farting." It's kind of offensive to the recipient. The "stench" doesn't exactly make us want to respond in a positive way. Usually, we would want to move away from the "fart." But what if that person and their fart just kept following you around, or worse yet, got right in your face and really let one loose? Wouldn't you want to say, "Hey, leave me alone; I haven't done anything to you!" Herein lies the next lesson of grounding through the heart rather than reacting to the fart.

In chapter six, I shared a meditation on grounding through love in the heart. This meditation is a very powerful one to return to as much as you need. If you meditate with this or any other heart-grounding meditation everyday for the next month, you will really start living the change in your life much more consistently. You will begin to feel a noticeable shift. It will become harder to throw yourself off balance. It would be a small fifteen-minute investment of your day with a huge return.

I suggest doing this meditation before you start your day. We are just as bombarded by a myriad of ripples as we are the multitude of radio and electromagnetic waves in our environment every day. In fact, even our ripples are electromagnetic waves since we ourselves are electromagnetic energy. Each day when we go out into the world, we are confronted with negative energy ripples from unconscious people. You wouldn't go to work naked, right? Think of morning meditation as "dressing" for your spirit and your energy to protect you from the "harsh elements."

You could also be that person on a given day. This is because we all go in and out from time to time as negativity will create new oil spills, and we lose our connection to the true source. So, yet again, we return to the refinery to recover ourselves and return to our heart center where our divine umbilical cord of light connects us to our creator.

These day-to-day spills that cause us to go in and out are like sparks on the original spills that began in childhood when your original birth self, Clarity, first became confused. They stoke and provoke these old spills, and we get smoked into our own unclear vision. The next thing you know, we are like drunk drivers driving under the influence of old negative pain, or driving while intoxicated by the hurt and anger of our unresolved hearts.

When we react to someone and lose our grounding in the heart, it is because there is still an unresolved piece of our past emotional hurts stored in our cells that get agitated by the fiery sparks of others. A spark blows our way while we are peacefully eating our marshmallows by our tents, pitched at the "KOA Ego Campground" situated on "Lost River." "Hey, who blew that spark into my marshmallow?"

You can easily access these old hurts by noticing your repeat lines of negativity, the ones that put you or others around you down. We can call this a game of, "What's Your Line?" These lines can be inwardly or outwardly directed and typically sound like,

- "Oh, I'm no good, and no one will love me."
- "I am unworthy."
- "It doesn't matter what I say, I don't count."
- "People ignore me."
- "I'm the only one that knows anything around here."
- "I can't count on anyone because people let me down."
- "People don't own their stuff."
- "See, people are really stupid, so I must take matters into my own hands."

These are the lines of the hurt self that we must bring into the heart for healing. They have become our self-fulfilling prophesies from which we create scenarios to prove them. We are then crooked lawyers gathering the evidence to support the claim.

We must then re*fine* ourselves yet again and, as we do this, we re-*find* ourselves. The oil stains are then cleared from the beautiful, spectral waters of our divine selves. So then, when you look in the mirror, Clarity smiles back at you and you and she are one again.

The heart meditation serves as a shield that protects you from the negativity and psychological farts around you. It will help you stay centered in your heart and not fall back into old hurts from the inflicted negative sparks of others that agitate your oil. I'm not saying you won't be agitated, but you will be able to remember to breathe and stay grounded in the heart more quickly.

The more you do the meditation, the much more quickly and easily you will be able to return to the heart. Remember the emotional muscle. The more you go back with repetition, the more the muscle finds comfort in its much healthier and stronger place. This is very healing, because at some point you will find that your oil doesn't get agitated anymore. Do you want to know why? Because your oil is finally resolved and you are now living fully in your God-given, Clarity self!

What an ultimate divine gift to you...and humanity. What an ultimate gift to Mother Earth herself. The more we are grounded in the heart, the more we will want to avoid destructive acts. If there is no destructiveness remaining in ourselves, we cannot project destructiveness into the world, period!

Another simple tool, in addition to the heart meditation, can be carried in your treasure chest of protection toward going out in the world. It will help you stay grounded even in the face of repetitive farts. This takes only a moment and can be done every morning before you start your day. I learned this from one of the great teachers I have had in my life, a Native American healer who helped me through many of my own soul lessons.

First, identify the way you typically refer to God. You may say "God," "Divine Source," "Father," "Great Spirit," or whatever feels most right for you. Stand up and take a few breaths: clearing, slow, and deep. Spread your arms out and upward and say, "Great Spirit, Father, it is I, (fill your name in), your daughter/son. Please fill me with what I need for this day." Hold your arms out, keep breathing slowly, and feel anything that may be coming in. You may get a message, or see an image, or it may be silent without an image and that is okay, too. Then bring your hands down in toward your solar plexus and bring the energy in by connecting with both hands to your solar plexus to ground the energy there. We bring this energy into the solar plexus because that is our power center. In martial arts, it is called the *dantian*. As you bring your hands in, try to sense the edges of the energy field. You may feel a slight density with a force in it. Thank the Great Spirit for his offerings to you.

Next say, "Earth Mother, it is I, (fill in your name), your daughter/son. Please fill me with what I need for this day." Outstretch your arms again, this time more toward the earth to receive. Breathe in and out slowly and deeply and listen for any messages. Be receptive to any images or just pause in the silence. Be with the moment and take in whatever comes to you. Then bring your hands in again toward your solar plexus, imagining the edges of the energy as you connect with your hands to the solar plexus. Thank the Earth Mother for her offerings to you. Take note of how you are feeling. You are now ready to step out into the day.

Any reactions we have to another's oil can only occur if we have not resolved and therefore are living out of the original core wound oil in ourselves. Our core wound oil is reflected in our repeat lines, usually derived very early in life. Once we are truly grounded in the heart, and thus resolved of our original oil core wounds, anyone else's oil will just be like water off a duck's back. And I salute you in a joyful quack!

Now, I invite you to go deeper with a guided meditation to clear those old negative tapes even more completely. To prepare for this meditation, first identify your strongest negative line, the one that comes back to you most repeatedly in your life. You will know it because this is the one that causes you to feel your lowest, most sad, or angriest and will show up at those moments. This one usually starts with, "See…" and feels like a statement to prove a perceived point that angers or despairs you. It may be inwardly directed or outwardly directed like the examples I shared earlier. Take a moment now to identify this line.

When you have this line, please refer to the box on the following page entitled, "Clearing Old Tapes," to do this meditation. Like the other guided meditations in this book, this is available on my website, *www.ultimate-healing.com*, as an audio download for your ease of meditating.

CLEARING OLD TAPES

Get comfortable and start consciously breathing in more slowly and exhaling slowly and deeply, and again breathing in slowly and exhaling slowly and deeply, and again breathing in and exhaling slowly and deeply.

Now, connect as far back as you can to the first time in your life you remember thinking and feeling your most repeated oil-stained line. Identify that early scene. What was happening? Who was there at this moment that you had the feeling for the first time? What else do you see in the scene? Can you hear what anyone is saying? Where are you as a child in the scene?

Breathe and notice... breathe and listen... breathe and connect with what your younger self was feeling as you see the drama play out. How old are you? Connect with what your child self was feeling at the time of this original hurt. Feel the emotions of your child self connected with the hurt as you see this memory through your child self.

As you identify this hurt in your child self and how it is making your child self feel, put your hand over your heart and stay connected with your child self's heart.

Breathe... relax.... breathe.... Breathe slowly in and out. What is the hurt line your child self is feeling? Hear the words of your child self's hurt. Now focus on the many ways you have recreated this hurt feeling in your life with other scenes. Notice that the players may be different and the scenes may be different, but the emotional hurt you are re-experiencing is the same. Feel the negative emotional charge or possible resentments connected with this recurring hurt. Notice in your body where you are carrying the pain.

Now, give this emotional pain a visual image. For instance, it may look like coal, rocks, or mud. It may have a certain color or texture. Whatever comes into your mind to visually represent the pain will be correct for you. Continue to breathe in and breathe out consciously. As you keep your hand over your heart, accept that you are helping the pain and emotions from these memories to leave your body.

As you continue breathing slowly in and out, imagine a divine breath from a guardian angel in the heavens breathing into you. Imagine this angelic breath coming in through your crown chakra and descending into that part of your body where the pain has been stored. As this divine, angelic breath comes into that area, it begins to break up this emotional pain. On your outward breath, as the angel's breath continues to assist you and breathe with you, imagine your visual image of the pain breaking up and disintegrating. With every inward breath, as the angel's breath comes into you, the pain disintegrates into smaller and smaller pieces. With every outward breath, the pieces leave you.

Continue to breathe in and out as you imagine this old pain disappearing out of you. You see the pieces shoot up into the heavens and disappear into God's light for final healing. Keep breathing and watching the pieces disintegrate and go upward into the heavens. They disappear high up into the light until there are no more pieces left to send up. Feel your heart, and the heart of your child self that you are connected with, opening. Release any tears that are present as you feel your hearts, together, open in love.

The earlier heart meditation grounds us in the heart and provides us with a shield as we go out into the day. The power center visualization grounds us into our solar plexus for the day as we bring down the energies of the Great Spirit and bring up the energies of Mother Earth into our core. It further supports our ability to stay grounded in the heart. Both of these are great tools to help us to not get knocked off balance, kind of like an "emotional" *dantian* for our heart power center. The last meditation helps us clear our old negative tapes at a deeper level, which helps us to not distract ourselves from the heart and become confused by the small, scared self.

Now, as you innocently walk through your life and get farted on, you have a field of protection that will help keep you grounded and steady as you move through the wide mix of energies of the day. Remember, the extent to which you have old oil that has not been cleansed and healed is the extent that you are at risk for reacting to someone else's oil. Always know that any reaction to another person is a reaction to your own self, period.

It is true and inescapable that when you get this, you will no longer be dependent on other people to get it right, for you now have your well-being intact. Then you get to send out all those wonderful, wonderful ripples—the kind that can even heal the heart of any person who is hurtful to you.

Chapter Twenty-Four

The Divine Billboards of Grace

The essential truths for ultimate living and ultimate healing, which I have presented in this book so far, are amplified in another emotionally challenging story from my life. I will illustrate the important soul lessons of these essential truths as they occur within the chapters of this story. Along the way, I will also point out some very powerful synchronicities that have marked this event in my life.

The story begins on a beautiful day. Unsuspecting, I was about to become the recipient of a particularly disturbing fart. The sun was shining brightly and Sister Grace walked in, but I didn't know it, of course. If I had, I might have made other plans! I'm sure glad I didn't because I really don't want to miss the beautiful lessons from Sister Grace. Without a doubt, she would have gotten me on another day anyway because of her deep love and her desire for our total healing.

The night before, I was at a bookstore with my mother and went to get us a table at the café. I noticed a book on the table, *Zero Limits, The Secret Hawaiian System for Wealth, Health, Peace & More* (John Wiley & Sons, Inc., 2007) by Joe Vitale and Ihaleakala Hew Len, Ph.D. I had never heard of the book, so I curiously picked it up. It was about an ancient Hawaiian system of healing through forgiveness and releasing negative energy called *ho'oponopono*.

In the book, Joe Vitale shares his conversations with Dr. Len, who was teaching him the principles of *ho'oponopono*. To begin with, Dr. Len explains, we are responsible for everything in our lives—every circumstance and every outcome.[21] Okay, I could buy that, but then Dr. Len explains to Joe Vitale further that we are responsible for everyone else's lives, because the entire world is our creation. In *ho'oponopono*, if you take full responsibility for your life, then everything you experience is your cause and your responsibility to heal.[22] Hmm, I'm all about self-responsibility but, wow, am I responsible for everyone else, their actions, behaviors, and outcomes?? I had to buy the book.

That night when I got home, I couldn't wait to read a little more. When I awoke the next morning, I felt an immediate and strong connection to what I had read so far. I wasn't used to a book greeting me before my morning coffee! Still, I couldn't let my morning coffee be upstaged, so I went to the local diner and decided to read and have my breakfast. That wasn't working very well, and being a perfect summer day, I spontaneously decided that this book was worth a day at Rehoboth Beach, about a two-hour drive from Baltimore. I don't remember having ever been so compelled to read a book.

So, off I went and Grace went with me. I could have known because the synchronicities were shining more than ever. They were actually popping out left and right. The last time they had felt so strong was during the healing fire over twenty years ago. I was on almost a natural high. I concluded that the synchronicities were this strong because the book must be holding some extremely powerful points for my life. I was more correct than I could have known.

I got caught in some major traffic jams on the way, and I was stopped completely for half-hour segments a few times. I decided to read more of the book during those jams, not knowing that the traffic jams themselves and the many synchronicities along the ride were signifying much more than a perfect book for me. I did not know of the coming "jam" I was about to create in my own life as I waited out the traffic jams.

Perfect day! Even the billboards were talking to me with synchronous messages. One of them said, "Heaven or hell, choose better health, live beautifully." I flashed back to my history with gambling challenges and reconnected. I had always felt the "hell" of gambling and yearned for the "heaven" of feeling free from its addictive constraints. Then there is the parallel of original addiction and the fear-based thoughts of the small self. Better health equals better thoughts and beautiful living.

During one of the "jams," I was reading that there is nothing but divinity and that from divinity we receive inspiration.[23] I looked up from the book and immediately saw a billboard advertising the First Baptist Church and a line that said to accept Christ's divinity!

Traffic remained at a standstill, so in amazement I continued reading until the traffic began to move. I inched along again, and the next billboard came into view. It read, "Love choices?" and had an accompanying picture of lotto tickets. The very next billboard behind that said, "Clear Channel," and underneath it said "Delaware lottery." Oh my! In my mind's eye, I immediately flashed into my long and challenging recovery from gambling addiction, most of which occurred in Delaware casinos. My recovery can be described as "clearing my channels." I was still moving through the energetic urges to gamble at that time and had to be attuned to relapse risks.

This astounding car ride continued. It was beginning to feel like a ride of my life in review. I pulled over to use a bathroom. Unbelievably, the billboard at the turn-off read, "#1 choice, Delaware beaches, the money you could be saving!" Next to that, a billboard read, "Art, by house." Being an artist, I was acutely aware of the diametrically opposed energies of addiction and art—addiction causes a disconnection from self, and art facilitates a connection to one's pure creative, divine self. To me, "art" paired with "house" signified the way *home* for me through the divinity of creativity. My creative energy had been a tremendous healing force to resolve addiction in my life.

I began excitedly writing these "life review" billboard messages on a napkin as they occurred while I continued in the traffic jam. Sister Grace, in full stride, provided them one after another. It was as if she was running ahead of my car to place another and another! Plus, she was juxtaposing fear-based gambling messages with love-based spiritual messages. Grace does not tire!

I received one more surprise just now as I am sharing this story with you. I looked at the napkin I had saved for the past two years since that amazing, Grace-infused day. There must have been a part of me that knew I would eventually be writing this, because I had scribbled, "You must become your own guru." Next to that I had written that a title for one of the chapters in my book should be "Becoming 'Guru'"! I had known I wanted to write, but I just didn't know at the time that the messages on the billboards that day would become part of my book—and part of the lesson toward becoming my own guru.

Chapter Twenty-Five

Ungrounded in the Fart

I arrived at the beach late, unaware that I was soon to experience one of the biggest soul-stirring "jams" of my life. I was still in a wonderfully elated state of mind from my magical ride. Some daylight still remained, and I had already decided by this point that I would spend the night.

I set my intention on a great parking space and drove down to the bottom of the road where it met the beach on the main drag. "Oh, perfect day! Look, a spot right down at the bottom!" Someone had just gotten into their car to pull out. "Lucky me," I thought, "I'm the next car coming." I stopped and put a blinker on, but the spot was straight ahead, not really on the left or right. I figured a blinker would still be a signal for the car behind me that I was waiting for a spot.

All of a sudden, I heard someone yelling angrily behind me. I looked in my rearview mirror. A very young seasonal police officer was the source of the yelling. (*Oh, mirror, mirror, on the wall, who's the angriest of them all?*) All of this yelling confused me. I didn't realize he was directing his yelling at me, and could not even understand what he was yelling about. I didn't like the smell of this puppy!

His volume increased and there was so much anger in his

voice; I was taken aback. I was confused. I tuned in more as he spewed and sputtered, "Keep moving, keep moving, I told you, you are blocking traffic!" "Huhhhh? He must not realize that I am waiting for a parking spot," I surmised. Still grounded, I kindly turned my head back toward him and said, "Officer, I can't keep moving. I'm waiting for a parking spot." He blew a psychological anal gasket and bellowed, practically spitting as he farted, "[Pffffft, pffffffft!] Keep moving, keep moving, I told you!"

I stayed emotionally grounded, but I really wanted this perfect parking spot. So, in a kindly voice, I tried again, "Officer, where would you like me to pull over so that I can have this spot?"

Though I tried to be kind with my words, I was unaware that I was starting to lose my ground. Unknown to me was the inner churning of my own not yet formed "pfffffft," a quiet rumbling that I did not yet detect. I was starting to feel the need to "let one" and I didn't know it. Oh, boy! The rumbling started to build and I awaited his response. I think he was about to burst a blood vessel with the magnitude of his, pffffffffft, yelling as he bellowed the same words again with blood-vessel-bursting volume, "YOU ARE BLOCKING TRAFFIC; KEEP MOVING NOW!"

He was more right than he knew and more than I realized. It wasn't so much the traffic flow at the beach, but my own divine flow that I was starting to block. Otherwise, the next thing out of my very-soon-to-be-farty mouth would not have been so unkind. I heard myself thinking, "Is there some kind of law against waiting for a parking spot?" I rumbled and churned. But I knew I had to obey and keep the car moving; in that moment I got utterly jammed up. No longer in my grounded state and allowing myself to become bowled over by his noxious gas, I farted an audible, "[Pfffffft.] Fuck you," as I pulled away. I immediately realized, "Oh, shit, now look what you've done, Caren!"

As I moved on, I quickly approached a traffic jam only about a block up. Kind of poetic, isn't it? Jam meets jam! We were in the pinnacle moment, Grace in full orchestration, as I moved through the following God-loving agony. I looked behind me and saw that the officer was still standing from where I drove off. I thought, "Wow, did I just actually get away with that?" But our full-blown version of *Fart Wars* was not over.

All of a sudden, the officer took off in a very fast run as if I was a hardened criminal. When he got up to my car, I had the window down and was ready for him. Surely a sincere apology would help, I anticipated. "Officer, I am so sorry. Please accept my apology. That was very wrong of me to say to you." He yelled, as if I had said nothing, "Take your keys out of the ignition and put them on the seat beside you." I tried to speak kind words again as I did what he commanded, "Officer, I am so sorry. I've been very stressed. I came here to unwind and I let my stress get the best of me. Please accept my apology."

The next line that bellowed out of him sent a wave of terror through me, "You tried to run me over back there!" he continued to yell and burst his veins. I was terrified and shaking at this point as I responded, shocked, "Officer, I did not try to run you over. When I realized that you would not allow me to wait for the parking spot, I kept moving like you told me to, but I did not try to run you over!"

He offered no acknowledgement as he retorted, "Open the door and get out of your car!" Hmm, I thought hopefully, "Maybe he just thinks I'm drunk, and he's going to give me a test. As soon as he sees that I'm sober, everything will be fine, right?" I got out of the car and he commanded me to turn and face the car.

Whoaaa, I don't watch much television, but I figured I was about to be searched. I put my hands on the roof because I thought I had seen that on TV. Not what he wanted. He screamed at me, "Put your hands behind your back!"

I was shaking so hard, I don't think I'd ever been so scared in my life. I heard him yell the next utterly unbelievable lines, "You are under arrest! You have the right to remain silent. (I sure wished I had remained silent a little earlier.) You are being charged with two felonies and a misdemeanor. You are being charged with reckless endangerment with possibility of death, attempting to flee the scene against the command of an officer, and disorderly conduct due to blocking vehicular traffic. You are also receiving a citation for failure to produce a current insurance card." (My current card, unbeknownst to me, had expired and I didn't have the new one with me.)

The next thing I knew, he pushed me into the backseat of the police car, handcuffed, and took me to booking. Isn't that what they call it? Not the kind of book I thought I had signed up for that day. What happened to my wonderful book that I was going to read at the beach? I hadn't realized it by that point, but I was going to be living the lessons in that book, as an emotional lifeline to me very soon. I didn't know it was also a "virtual" book that would take on dimensionality in my life at that time.

Next, I was sent into a room with benches. A young guy was in there who was handcuffed to a bench. The officer led me to another bench, and I noticed that they all had metal rings attached to them. He then handcuffed me to one of the rings.

(*With this ring, I thee wed; I've committed my crime and made my bed.*) Though I didn't think the "crimes" I had committed were valid, I had committed a crime against my heart where my divine, connected self lives and breathes the love that I knew.

∞∞∞∞∞∞∞∞∞∞∞∞∞∞∞

I have said to clients at times, "Yeah, wouldn't it be nice if we could give people psychology citations for when they psychologically fart on us and then they could be ordered to x number of therapy sessions?" You may chuckle. My clients and I do, as it is said in good fun.

But let's not forget that the only farts we are responsible for are our own. The ripples rule. We must own our ripples and take our part on the heart-grounded side where we infuse our ripples with love. Then, in truly healing ourselves—and ultimately the world—we would not have to play *Fart Wars* anymore! As a result, we would have played at the risk of our transformation and won!

I didn't win that day. There were lessons to be learned.

Chapter Twenty-Six

This is Not a Game of Shame

Do you think I'm being a bit hard on myself in my interpretation of this incident and my stated crime against the heart? Remember the lessons of the soul. This is not about self-deprecation. If it were, I would never have been ready or able to tell this life story or any of the soul-lesson stories I have told in this book in a way that honors and teaches the healing of the heart. It is quite the opposite of self-deprecation, my dear readers. It is born out of the fact that I honor my soul lessons.

The greatest intention in my life is to be able to send out the purest love-based ripples that I can, as I honor my journey and the journey of all of my blessed fellow travelers. The second greatest intention in my life is my hope that these soul lessons from my journey can also touch you directly and ignite the same ultimate desire within you. There is truly no deeper healing than the healing of our hearts—that which I am sharing with you now. This is why we must lose the shame and face our reflection and all of its distortions with love.

I do not want to elicit sympathy from you. You should not want to elicit sympathy at any time through your life when you have a difficult emotional experience. Sympathy puts us in a place of disempowerment. It can also block us from understanding our own role and responsibility in the situations we co-create. We all play a part, so no matter how out of balance another person may seem to you, you participate in, choose, and create every one of your life scenarios. We may certainly feel compassion for each other as we exchange our challenging life stories—for that is based out of love, not out of the need to rescue and commiserate.

We each draw all of our experiences. If we don't recognize this, and are only focused on the behavior of another person, we are then lost in victimization. We are not in our power; we are therefore lost in our small, fear-based selves, and are at risk for missing the soul lessons we have set up in those experiences. We can consider how changing our own responses or even the subtle energies of our responses may have a changing effect on the other.

We are only responsible for our own ripples. This is how we heal ourselves and the world. We do not heal ourselves and the world by focusing hyper-vigilantly on our opinions of the bad behaviors of others. I often say to my clients that the best way to change another is to change oneself.

My journey is the same journey we are all on—the journey home, to the truest home, where we ground ourselves in the pure divine light of the heart. We have all had a piece of this desire to control the world around us since we have all lived much of our journey out of unconscious projections of fear and the scared small self. We all need to make the thirteen-inch journey from our heads to the pure divinity of our hearts. Give yourself a moment to identify yet again how you have played this out in your own life.

Then, take in these next direly important words. This is *not* a journey of shame and self-effacement. Instead, this *is* the transformation we seek. It is the transformation of truly being able to look squarely at ourselves and face our soul lessons without fear.

This is with a reflection of self-love as we realize the beautiful beings of light that we truly are. This is the ultimate healing that allows us to send out the purest, love-based ripples. They become the full spectrum of crystalline ripples of love because they are born out of the waters of Clarity. I have reflected our choice to step into our divine true selves in the following poem, "Triumph in the Relative Ballroom":

In a matter of minutes I could be in lost-self or divine.
One would slip away, the other would dance its glory dance
leading my soul around the relative ballroom.

They both dance passion, but one will trample your spirit,
suffocate your soul. Then when you're a shell echoing its call,
it will shape-shift, declaring itself as you.
And funny, you never noticed the moments stolen
and the present raped from you.

The other, if given a chance, ignites you into a foxtrot swing,
bursts your kundalini open so you can be fresh and vibrant.
All colors alive and expressing, it emerges from your soul
and dearly thanks you for your acknowledgment,
like a jack-in-the-box, coy and hidden, but only in need
of an invitation to spring forth its life-bursting energy,

as if to say,
"I'm here, here I am, in the red beginning.
Dance with me in abandon, and I will share with you
all my God-given glorious colors."

I encourage you to write a poem from your old scared oil-stained self. Then write a poem from your higher, divinely connected self. In connecting in this creative manner, everything you need is always there for you to access. Your higher-knowing self needs only to be invited. If you give yourself a chance with this, you may be surprised at what comes through you. You may notice how the words and emotional energy evoked from each of the poems are dissimilar and affect you differently. The experience can be very powerful in integrating this vital difference in orienting ourselves through love rather than shame.

This is so very important because as I tell the "parking space" story further, I want you to feel the love in my heart, so that you can feel the love in your heart, as I embrace these soul lessons. I want for you to be able to connect with that love because I want for you to no longer be afraid. You will then be able to expose the self-created illusions of Coyote, the master trickster, and no longer succumb to his trickery. I want to help you feel that you are already a beautiful and radiant being filled with divine light and love. There is nothing to "fix" because you are not defective. There is only the highest honor you can bestow upon yourself and the world, that of self-accountability and your responsibility to yourself and everyone else to fully step in.

I am aware of how many times in this book I repeat this to you. But many times in your life, it is likely that you have lived out of your small addicted self and its unconscious projected fears. We are doing soul-level reprogramming here. Just know that every time you consider and go deeper with these lovingly true words, it will deepen the groove of higher truth within you. Soon enough, the new groove will be deeper than the small, fear-addicted self's groove. Then your personal transformation will skyrocket!

∞∞∞∞∞∞∞∞∞∞∞∞∞∞∞

My "parking space" story and the Grace-infused lessons continued to line up.

Chapter Twenty-Seven
Ultimate Healing

While I sat in the detention room cuffed to the bench, an officer told me that I would be fingerprinted and photographed. After that, the young man who was handcuffed across the room tried to converse with me, "Hey, what are you in here for?" I was still shell-shocked as I looked down instead of answering.

I had to settle my spirit a bit; the book that I was so eager to read came back into my thoughts. Though I had only gotten fifty pages into it before jam met jam, I was starting to grasp what the authors were saying. If the guiding principles of *ho'oponopono* were correct, then that meant I was responsible for the police officer's anger. It even meant that I was responsible for this young man who sat in the detention room with me, and whatever he had done to land here on this bench across from me! Oh my, but it was so much to take in! Still I quieted my uncertain voice and thought about the police officer. I remembered that in the book, Dr. Len explained we must ask over and over again for forgiveness for everything we have caused in others and then state our love to them.[21]

Woweeee, this was tough, and it was pushing against my hardwood ego grain big time, but here goes. After all, I found this book very compelling. So, in my heart I asked the officer for forgiveness in what I had caused in him and told him I loved him. Right away, upon doing and feeling this, I found myself imagining his childhood, not that I really personally knew his childhood. I just closed my eyes and allowed myself to start imagining...

He was a little boy and he was riding his tricycle up and down his childhood street. He was alone and he seemed very, very sad. I reached into his heart to hear his story as I continued to view the scene.

His father put him down all the time unceasingly. He was an unremitting, very, very angry man. His father was extremely verbally abusive and quite often beat him for no apparent reason.

The child officer was a very good boy; he tried everything to please his daddy and could not figure out why his daddy was always angry at him. He concluded that there must be something wrong with him as he swallowed through a knot in his throat. He rode his bike up and down, up and down, trying to find the road to make his father happy.

I felt a sudden welling of compassion for this officer as I then imagined the huge pain of internalized anger he had carried around in his spirit. I sat with this feeling for a little while before I opened my eyes.

I looked up and said to the young man across the room, "So what are *you* here for?"

He was quite a lighthearted one, and chuckled as he said to me, "Ohhhh, so now you're talking!" He then told me that he was with a friend who had shoplifted. He tried to tell his friend not to do it, but they both ended up getting arrested for it.

∞∞∞∞∞∞∞∞∞∞∞∞∞∞∞∞

Regardless of whether this was literally true or not, what was dawning on me by this point was *ho'oponopono* is a way of looking deeper into the ripple effect. Since the negative ripples that we send out have a collective effect on all of us, we are utterly responsible for everyone else's behavior, not just our own. I began to understand more completely this far-reaching truth:

in our own behaviors, we energetically influence and affect the behaviors of others, regardless of whether we ever meet them. In this way, yes, I caused the officer's anger. I even caused the young man's poor judgment, though I did not know him when he made his mistake.

As I grasped this truth about our collective energy, my heart opened! I began to feel more deeply than ever the divine oneness that we are, and realize more comprehensively that there is no separation. No exceptions! We are all one cause and we are all one effect! What we do to ourselves, we inescapably do to one another. I faced this shamelessly and without self-deprecation, as I released anger and despair on a level that I did not even know I had carried, and I fell in love. I rippled with love and felt the waking up of ultimate healing within me and toward the collective whole.

I never did learn the name of the young man in the detention room with me, so I will call him "Danny." I chose this name because a popular interpretation of this name is "God is my judge." I interpret that to mean that divine love is the judge.

∞∞∞∞∞∞∞∞∞∞∞∞∞∞∞

"So, what are *you* here for," he asked me again? I gave him a play-by-play of what happened, and he quickly and gladly came to my rescue cursing out officers for me! His innocent humor and kind intention was a trickle of comic relief. I smiled in the irony and chuckled. We were both quiet at this point.

An interesting scene then followed with this young man as he angrily muttered, "This place is driving me crazy! I can't stand it in here! I'm so bored, I'm going crazy!" He proceeded to kick a chair within leg's reach, so hard that it upended. This attracted an officer into the room who yelled at him and warned him to not do it again. After the officer left the room, I watched in humorous amazement as my new clown friend tried to get off of the bench, still handcuffed by one hand, and do push-ups.

In all likelihood, he did not consciously know that he was trying to physically ground the energy of his anger. Such negative energy has to go somewhere, so in this limited environment he was doing his best to release it without causing himself a further problem. Danny continued his attempts to do his one-handed push-ups while he was still handcuffed to the bench. In the midst of his effort, he ranted and raved, complaining about how hard it was for him to sit still. Even though a good effort, his one-handed push-ups were frustrating him rather than helping him with his boredom and unsettledness.

I smiled as I watched and offered him sympathetic condolences. "I can relate. It is hard to sit here all this time. How long have you been in here?" He belted out, "More than five hours." I had been there only about an hour.

"Wow. You know, I'm a therapist back home and I happened to be trained in ADHD, and it sounds like you might be going through some of the stuff that people with that challenge do. Would you like some tips?" He said yes, and vehemently repeated that he can't stand being stuck in one place, just waiting with nothing to do. I offered to him some breathing exercises to ground him and he seemed receptive. Our conversation about this seemed to help him as he collected himself on the bench. We continued talking. Grace had provided me some relief in this high-wire learning trauma where balance certainly mattered, with the presence of my new clown friend.

I needed to use the toilet, which was in a set-apart alcove in the same room. An officer uncuffed me and stood nearby. I couldn't help but notice a wrapped toilet paper roll right by my side that indicated that the brand name was "Encore." Cute, Grace! I was definitely not planning a repeat performance!

By 8:00 p.m. that night, I was escorted to a conference room where the magistrate of Georgetown, Delaware, could see me via closed-circuit television. I had to state my version of what had happened; she had already reviewed the police officer's statement. I did my best to hold my composure; I knew from my young friend that the decision she made would determine whether I would be released on bail or whether I would have to spend the next few days in jail awaiting my hearing.

I explained my version to the magistrate who noted that I was calm and cooperative. Because I was an out-of-towner and because I had assaulted a police officer, she decided to release me on bail, but at a higher bail of $5,000. She then explained that I would not be allowed to use a credit card. Oh dear. Most of us don't walk around with $5,000.

I was allowed to make a phone call to ask someone to bail me out. The police had confiscated my cell phone with all of my phone numbers. The only numbers I knew by heart were my parents', the two people in my life who had my best interest at heart. I knew they were out of town at their summer home. I made the call knowing that I would have to immediately extinguish their fear when they heard my voice. "Mom and Dad, don't worry. I'm ok, I'm not hurt, but you need to drop everything and drive to Rehoboth right now because I've been arrested."

I felt such shame and embarrassment in the moment. But they responded in this call as they always have, with loving reassurance, compassion, and non-judgment. God bless them; they were already offering to pay for my lawyer, find me the best lawyer—whatever I needed. I thanked them for their loving support and told them we could talk about it all later. I reassured them that I would be safe driving home once I was allowed to leave. Interrupting the call, an officer came in, and said the judge changed her mind, that I was allowed to pay by credit card.

∞∞∞∞∞∞∞∞∞∞∞∞∞∞∞

In looking back, I know that Sister Grace had allowed me that call to my parents; it brought me a moment of loving relief, a saving grace to buffer my distress, as I completed the transaction. Grace, though fierce in her love, loves us enough to buffer the road with her saving graces while we navigate through the necessary bumps. In this way, she calms our spirits and nurtures us through these painful times. I appreciate more and more the value and gift of these saving graces to ease the pain of traumas as I move through my more difficult soul lessons.

∞∞∞∞∞∞∞∞∞∞∞∞∞∞∞

Next, I was taken to Georgetown, Delaware, to pay my bail,

fully appreciating the permission I was granted to pay $5,000 by credit card to keep my butt out of jail. On the way back to Rehoboth, the female police officer who escorted me realized that I was not a hardened criminal, and she uncuffed me after four hours of wearing this lovely double bracelet-in-one. On her police radio though, at one point, I heard her say she was transporting "the criminal" to Georgetown. I wasn't in a position to correct her.

∞∞∞∞∞∞∞∞∞∞∞∞∞∞∞

I began to think, a "criminal" steals what is not his or hers, whether it is money, power, or control from the victim. To that end, most of us have had a criminal in our spirits at least occasionally that has needed love and healing. Any time we are not grounded in the heart and we are acting out of an emotional fart, the small self has gassed us in fear again and stolen our show. Though unaware and not consciously intended, the lost, addicted, small ego self, fearing annihilation, tries to rob the true divine self of its throne.

And yet again, my dear friends, remember and practice this: we must love that hurt self right into our hearts where the ultimate healing can occur. Think about this. What happens when a distressed or scared child feels nurtured, supported, loved, and understood? That child does not act out anymore, but begins to settle and become more peaceful and quiet.

∞∞∞∞∞∞∞∞∞∞∞∞∞∞∞

On the way back from Georgetown, the officer escorted me to an ATM machine in a convenience store so that I could get cash, because soon I would be allowed to get my car out of impound—it was impounded since I didn't have the proper updated insurance card. Back to the police station in Rehoboth, I was allowed to call my insurance company which, lucky for me, was available twenty-four hours to have my current card faxed. So, with my new insurance card faxed to the police station, I was finally allowed to go home. One quick payment to the impound lot cashier and, wonder of wonders (*wow*); I was in my car driving home by eleven o'clock. Sister Grace provided yet another saving grace, since without my car I would be stuck in Rehoboth, having played my "get out of jail for $5,000" card, but with no car to drive as they held the monopoly.

∞∞∞∞∞∞∞∞∞∞∞∞∞∞∞∞

As I wrote this chapter during the writing retreat, I felt the need to suggest to you, my dear fellow soul travelers, to please remember to spend a moment or more in each day truly nurturing yourself in whatever way feels right for your spirit. Even five minutes of conscious, intentional self-nurturing can bring grounding and comfort to you. I felt the need to tell you to make yourself important—that you *are* important! Then I realized that I needed to honor my own advice and take a break. I am important enough to do that. So, I took a break with my fellow writers to have lunch.

When I returned, I remembered to connect with my angels and light beings of loving, divine creation. I asked them to be here with me and support me in this process. I closed my eyes and held a very special crystal in my hand that I had bought earlier on the trip. This crystal had travelled with me to some very amazing places. I held the crystal to my heart and invited my angels and loving light beings to be with me, and I thanked them for their unconditional love and support. But, since I was a little new at remembering to do this on a regular basis, I was still trying to remember the names of some of these beautiful light beings that I've heard others call into their hearts.

So, I did the best I could. I called, "Raphael, Gabriel, Michelangelo, oh, oh, I mean Michael." I chuckled at myself and then decided to invite Michelangelo in anyway because of my connection to sculpture as an artist, and of course I still invited Archangel Michael! Calling our angels is a form of self-nurturing and self-care because they are available to support us in the perfected love that they are. We only need to ask and quiet our spirits to receive.

Chapter Twenty-Eight

My Family of Angels

The next day was Sunday. My parents and brother came mid-morning to hear what happened. I am truly blessed to have been born into a family of angels. Even though they have their stuff to work out in life—as we all do—I can tell you that they are in truth unconditionally loving. Almost always, they come from the heart. They have been huge soul teachers and guides in my life. I am so deeply grateful to my beautiful and loving family! I have been further blessed with a loving niece and nephew and equally loving extended family. I seem to have attracted this as well in some of my dear friends.

∞∞∞∞∞∞∞∞∞∞∞∞∞∞∞∞

If you are connecting, as you read this, with those who have been unconditional loving supports in your life, you may want to offer a silent prayer of gratitude now for their blessings. To the extent that you have not had this, you may want to offer a prayer of healing for those who have hurt you—whether they ever let such loving energy in or not—you may experience healing in yourself through this letting go. In all cases, know that through self-love, you can guide yourself to the love of others.

∞∞∞∞∞∞∞∞∞∞∞∞∞∞∞∞

So my loving family supported me that day as they would have on any day and helped me re-establish my ground with their love. Their love helped infuse my heart with the confidence I needed for what lay ahead.

That evening I went to my office and cancelled all of my clients for the week from my private therapy practice. I knew I would have to interview lawyers and find my way toward good legal support. Not to mention, my preliminary hearing was scheduled for Thursday morning. I had to get busy. I told my clients I had a family emergency—since I am my own family—and cleared out my week. I truly did not know if I would be going to jail and, if so, for how long. I did not know if my career as I knew it had ended. If I was convicted, I knew my license to practice as a clinical social worker would be revoked. My heart was wrenched at the threat of losing my life work and its deep meaning. I felt as if I had betrayed my clients.

∞∞∞∞∞∞∞∞∞∞∞∞∞∞∞

The experience of writing these words reconnected me with the intensity of emotions and fear I experienced, at the time of this heart-wrenching experience of my life. I felt the need to stretch and take a breather. I honored that. As I caught a glimpse of myself in the bathroom mirror before I went bouncing back up the stairs to continue writing, I heard myself say, "You are getting more and more beautiful." We all become more and more beautiful as we resolve ourselves back to the heart, living in love. We become more beautiful because we become more of who we truly are. It is Clarity reflecting herself back to our vision.

When I returned to the room to rejoin my fellow writing friends, one of them, Keith, said to me "Hey, you look really good, like you just got revived!"

Celebrate yourself! I know that each and every one of you are becoming more and more beautiful, too, as you wake up and go to the refinery every day. You are becoming more beautiful as you refine yourself and lovingly tend to your soul work to reveal the true Clarity that you are. I'm thinking of words from an old Pink Floyd song, "Shine on you crazy diamond..."

Chapter Twenty-Nine

The Lifeguard

Still laden with distress, my brother helped me begin the process of finding a lawyer. He contacted an acquaintance of mine, also a lawyer, that I am very fond of. I hadn't known Dominick Garcia very well, but I always felt a very loving presence about him. Our offices had been in the same building on the same floor at one point in time. He had helped me once with the formalities of a lease agreement, and I really enjoyed knowing him for that amount of time.

I felt a little embarrassed because he didn't know me very well, but I trusted him and got the sense that he would be very supportive. He was exactly that; he gave me excellent legal advice and helped me on my path to find the right attorney. He explained that it would be best for me to be represented by a local lawyer in Georgetown, Delaware, where the preliminary hearing would be. He explained that someone who knew the judges and prosecuting attorneys and even had lunch with them would be best.

On Monday morning, I began my search on the Internet for local Georgetown lawyers. I had to do my best to feel this out on my own, but Dominick was there, another saving grace from Sister Grace, to answer any questions I may have. By mid-morning, I had my search down to two lawyers and set up appointments with them both for that afternoon. I appreciated this small grace from Sister Grace that I had gotten such quick appointments, and drove back to Georgetown to consult with them. The synchronicities were mostly quiet, at least early in the day, and I was grateful.

The first lawyer was the "bull." He conveyed great sympathy toward me. He believed my description of what had happened, emphatically stated that I was innocent, that none of the above should have happened, and that technically it is not illegal to curse at a police officer. He exclaimed that these seasonal officers needed to be taught a lesson. If I would be patient, he was very sure he could get me excused from all charges and found innocent. He said that the process would take a couple of months because first I would have to refuse a plea bargain and then it would likely go to a jury trial. Yikes! I wasn't sure if I had the emotional constitution to withstand such an elongated process and still be able to go back to work and serve my clients.

The second lawyer, Ron, is the one I hired. He said that he believed the integrity of my story, but that a jury trial is exactly what I should avoid because the "nice, conservative citizens" of Georgetown would hear my case. He continued that once they heard that I said "fuck you" to one of their own police officers they may find me guilty, not realizing the potential severity of the consequences to me. He said we should try for a plea bargain and that I had a very good chance for it. He understood that I could not accept an outcome with even one criminal conviction or even with just probation, due to the risk to my professional license.

Here is an amazing twist, though maybe not so uncommon in small towns. When I first told my story, Ron perked up when I gave him the name of the seasonal police officer. He excused himself, and behind me I saw him ruffling through old files. When he came back to his desk, he revealed that he thought the officer's name sounded familiar. He then explained that, in fact, he had represented that very police officer as his defense attorney when this officer was a juvenile and had gotten himself in trouble! He reassured me that this was not a conflict of interest and later, Dominick, my guardian-lawyer-angel friend, confirmed the same. I just hoped that Ron wasn't this guy's uncle or someone close in relation, being the small town that it was.

∞∞∞∞∞∞∞∞∞∞∞∞∞∞∞

I followed my gut feeling and really got a sense of trust from him, though I knew enough about Grace and her synchronicities to be careful with my interpretation. I felt that there must be a soul connection in this since Ron once defended the young officer where anger was the precipitator and now would be defending me where anger again was the issue.

There was something else about Ron that felt right to me, and it was quite a wink from Grace that I would not even consider ignoring. Ron had a side job as a lifeguard at Rehoboth Beach and had been doing this for very many years. The more Ron and I spoke, the more I understood that this was a passion of his. There was no doubt at that point, that I wanted a lifeguard as my attorney! So, Sister Grace sent me a saving grace as a "life-guard" in the form of an attorney.

∞∞∞∞∞∞∞∞∞∞∞∞∞∞∞

Before leaving Ron's office, he told me that all I had to do to resolve the insurance card traffic citation was to go to the judge's chambers in Rehoboth, ask to speak to him, and show my updated card to have the traffic charge removed. I decided to spend the night in Georgetown to see the judge in the morning. I arrived at the only hotel in the area I could find. The clerk behind the desk said, while getting my room key, "Hey, you look familiar. Don't I know you?"

"I don't think so," I replied; I did not recognize her. She continued, "Oh, well you look amazingly like the woman whose photo (mug shot) was on the news last night who tried to run over a police officer." I did my best to hide my shock and said, "Oh, yes, we all have doubles out there, don't we...?"

∞∞∞∞∞∞∞∞∞∞∞∞∞∞∞

I look back now as I write this to you, my dear readers, and realize the double meaning in this. Did you catch on to it, too? We all have a double in life, don't we? One of us sends out the negative destructive ripples of our fear-based, small selves and the other one sends out the positive love-infused ripples. We look the same on the outside, do we not?

∞∞∞∞∞∞∞∞∞∞∞∞∞∞∞∞

Feeling panicked and scared, I told the clerk that I had changed my mind—that I wanted to search for a better rate. I left the hotel, got to my car, and immediately called Ron in my distress and fear. He reassured me that this kind of thing was common in small towns where news reporters have little else to write about. He said in no way did this make my case any more serious. He told me to relax. I asked him if it was a bad idea to spend the night, because the judge's office was in the same police station in Rehoboth where I was originally taken.

I reminded him that I had also received a "no-contact order" from the police; I was not to come within fifty feet of the officer. He considered, and advised me that while it would probably be fine to stay, maybe I should go home and take care of this detail after the hearing instead. That is what I did.

I found out later that this news report was also broadcast on Fox 45, a station local to my residence. There was nothing I could do about that, though I felt fear around my anonymity regarding my clients. I knew many of them would understand, but what about those that didn't know me well? And what about when people name-searched me on the Internet to learn about their therapist or searched in general to find a therapist?

I felt hurt. Even though I understood the responsibility of personal accountability, feelings of "the punishment didn't fit the crime" gurgled inside of me.

∞∞∞∞∞∞∞∞∞∞∞∞∞∞

I had to just keep the faith that everything would work out in a good way and hold on to the fact that no matter what, we each define our own selves and who we really are. I knew that no one, no matter their opinions, defines who you are but you. I knew I had to uphold my own self in value or I would be allowing others to be mini-gods to me. I could not fear the opinions of others or I would be coming from fear and I would be back in the false confines of my small self.

Grace continued to send her synchronicities to me, and the news station, Fox 45, was no exception. I am starting to believe that synchronicities layer themselves in completed stacks as we resolve and complete a soul lesson. The magnitude of synchronicities perhaps equals the magnitude of the life lesson. It's as if we parallel our own lives, as dimensions of time fold up to meet themselves on the same point in a synchronous expression.

So, to explain, I will share the Native American meaning of "fox": when a fox enters your life in the unresolved state, there are lessons about visibility and figuring out your strategy. I sure felt exposed when I learned of the newscast. In addition, the fox also brings a message that you have been a wallflower in your own life and that you are worth noticing, or that you are watching yourself to prove to yourself that you exist."[24]

Given that I had come out of over a decade of gambling addiction and the isolation of that lifestyle where one can easily feel they have "disappeared," I was amazed when I looked up the meaning of the fox. Plus, as you know by now, any level of addiction includes small-self addiction. In this original addiction, we all "disappear" from who we really are. In the resolved state, the fox represents adaptability, observation, decisiveness, and integration.[25]

Coming home at the end of the day yesterday to work on book revisions, a fox crossed my path right as I turned into my street! This had happened in the past but it had been rare. I was hopeful that Grace would conclude that the lessons of this soul-stirring life chapter were complete, and that I had turned "fox" right side up in resolution.

From this point, the synchronicities of this emotionally traumatic life story intensified further. Grace had more in store and paid a visit yet again.

Chapter Thirty

Grace Followed Me Home

I hit a traffic jam where the entire road was closed! This was part of my route home, so I had to take a different road. My GPS kept sending me in a circle back to the same point. "Okay, Grace, I'm getting it!" I practically exclaimed out loud. It's time for me to take an entirely different route home in my life and my normal system of navigating is not working anymore. I had to stop the car, get out, and get help. If Grace could have put bells around the message and blew whistles, I believe she would have. It reminded me of a phrase I had heard that came from addiction recovery programs, "If you always do what you always did, you always get what you always got!" I had to continue integrating my lessons from this life chapter.

During the next couple of days, I worked on preparing myself mentally and emotionally for what lay ahead. At one point, while driving in my car—oh, what a ride it became yet again— Grace dealt me a huge synchronicity, challenging me to control the worst of my fears. A song came on the radio that most of us know well, though it is one I rarely hear. My mouth gaped open as Willie Nelson sang this old Paul Westmorland song. The title of it is "Detour" and the lyrics could not have matched better the situation I had created. The beginning lines are:

Detour, there's a muddy road ahead.
Detour, paid no mind to what it said.
Detour, oh, these bitter things I find.
Should have read that detour sign...

It continued on,

...trouble got in the trail.
Spent the next five years in jail.
Should have read that detour sign...

Almost shaking, I changed the station and tried to calm myself down.   I reminded myself that synchronicities do not necessarily predict outcomes as much as mark intense and significant learning moments in our lives. I started my conscious breathing to stay grounded, did my best to keep my focus on the present, and continued to work on being calm and not getting lost in my head.

During the same car ride, I had a conversation with my brother, Larry, who you may recall has been an unconditional loving support, guiding force, and angel in my life. He had been holding my hand and soothing my heart in the past few days. It was time for me to decide who I wanted to go with me to the court hearing. I knew that I did not want to go alone. My brother was ready to go if I wanted him to be my support there. In his natural, unconditional manner, he would meet me at the hotel after working very long hours to arrive by midnight.

At first, I did not want my parents to go. Without knowing the outcome, I felt protective of them. Incidentally, the fox is a protector of the family unit.[26] I decided that I would allow my parents to come because I could feel in their energy that they would have felt more helpless and distressed not being able to be there with me.

Chapter Thirty-One

Love Moves Mountains

On Wednesday I drove with my parents to Georgetown, Delaware, to spend the last evening with them before my court hearing. We relaxed on our way there and were quiet regarding the event about to unfold. After we were all settled into the room, my brother arrived around midnight as planned. We had gotten a large enough room for all of us, so there I was with my loving family of origin all around me.

∞∞∞∞∞∞∞∞∞∞∞∞∞∞∞∞

I cannot begin to describe the magnitude of incredible support I felt with all of us together in that space. I felt cradled as the energy of love in that room produced a strong vibration. If I were less afraid at that time, I believe that I would have consciously felt the vibration their love was producing and maybe even its tone, at the divine frequency of 528Hz, vibrating MI.

∞∞∞∞∞∞∞∞∞∞∞∞∞∞∞∞

We settled in for an hour or two more. This was so sweet, being the first time the four of us had spent the night under the same roof together since I was a child. Everyone was quiet. I was very nervous and trying to manage pangs of fear. Quietly, I tried to comfort myself with conscious breathing and thought about the guiding principles of *ho'oponopono*.

I breathed and anchored in my heart healing words of self-accountability to others and of asking forgiveness. I had hoped that somehow this would help me and everyone in that courtroom reach a state that would support a forgiving outcome. I prayed that this was meant to be and hoped for this saving grace from Sister Grace. Focusing on these healing words became a form of prayer that seemed to calm my spirit.

The next morning, we went to breakfast at the hotel. As I was sitting quietly doing my best to ground myself in prayer and positive affirmation, I felt the need to request something of my family that we used to do often in my childhood—and on rare occasions in the adult years that followed. I requested that we do an "Apple love-in."

Our last name is "Appel," but we are so used to being called "Apple" that we often would refer to ourselves that way. In my childhood, we used to have "Apple love-ins" where we would all four gather together in a circle, hug, and say out loud together in unison with joyful expression, "Apple love-in!" We would stand together having formed a "human apple." As we embraced, I truly think we all imagined the stem of the "apple" we formed. We would always chuckle right after. My father invented it and referred to it as "a circle of love of the family." So we did our Apple love-in there in the hotel lobby, and it was as joyful and heartfelt as always.

I asked for additional support from them—not to feel anger toward anyone in the courtroom, not even the police officer who arrested me. I shared with them my thoughts about the possible hurts in his life that may have propelled him to act out. I also shared about how we all create our own circumstances, and that we have a direct role in the behaviors and actions of others. I shared that rather than holding anger and animosity, if instead we wished him healing, that it would soften our own hearts and possibly his. They lovingly agreed.

I also asked them to send loving energy to the judge and attorneys, and overall just to hold that vibration of love. They all felt my words as I shared what they already knew, that there is no greater healing energy than love itself.

We met Ron at his office, and he gave us a quick briefing. He told us that the prosecuting attorney had a terrible reputation for not accepting plea bargains. Bluntly, my attorney called him an "ass" in his description to us. He said this guy was on a kick about prosecuting no matter what and that no one liked him. My family and I knew we had set the intent for love and that there was no more we could do but to have faith and keep centered in that love.

The hearing commenced and the prosecuting attorney accepted the plea bargain! All criminal charges were dropped and my sentence was reduced to a traffic violation and an agreement to attend one anger management class. My career was saved. I could go home to my work, my clients, my friends, my family, and my cats!

∞∞∞∞∞∞∞∞∞∞∞∞∞∞∞

I want to mention that I had reached out to my close friends earlier in preparation for a jury trial, since I didn't know for sure whether that would happen. I asked them to write letters for me attesting to my character and I received the grace of deeply loving responses. These loving friends wrote heartfelt statements about me as they have experienced me in their lives. I was joyfully overwhelmed by their acknowledgments!

I also received very kind loving support and character letters from three colleagues who gave without hesitation; this added even more to my feelings of gratitude and being loved. There were also a few closer clients with whom I had worked for a longer time. They knew me too well for me to have comfortably stayed with my "family emergency" explanation. I gave them a brief but more personal explanation of what had happened, asking nothing of them. What I received from all of them was unconditional acceptance of me and loving support.

I turn to you, my readers, and say, please reach out to the people you love who no doubt love you too in a time of need.

Do not make yourself small and undeserving of them giving you support, just as you would give it to them. Sometimes we have a habit of diminishing ourselves to try to be unburdening to the people we love, as if we are sparing them in some way. Of course, my friends, you have learned that you would be coming from your small, diminished self and not your true, divine self if you did that. You would also be depriving them of the love they would have ignited in themselves when you reached out for their giving. When we truly fall in love with our divinely-connected selves and return home to Clarity, we equally accept our roles as loving givers and worthy receivers.

∞∞∞∞∞∞∞∞∞∞∞∞∞∞∞

The day after the court hearing, I was so filled with love and appreciation for the overwhelming abundance of loving support, the only thing I wanted to do was go out and buy cards and gifts reflecting my gratitude. Of course I knew my family and friends would not feel I needed to do that, but I was so overjoyed with love that I simply had to.

While shopping for the gifts and cards that best reflected my feelings, I discovered some beautiful plaques with heartfelt phrases on them. One in particular caught my heart. Though I didn't buy it, I chose to write it down to personally remember it. It said, "If you think only sunshine brings happiness, then you have never danced in the rain!"

Later that evening after I arrived home, I heard my neighbors on their back porch socializing. They've often invited me to come over and spend neighborly time together and I have rarely taken them up on it, being the busy project person I am. In that moment, I couldn't think of a better thing to do but spend time with such fun-loving people, so I walked across the yard to join them. After a bit of cheerful relaxing, it started to rain. We all decided to relocate onto Dan and Jen's covered front porch.

We watched as quite a strong summer shower poured down, intoxicating us with uplifting ions. In that moment, another neighbor, Jenny, inquired to Jen, "Okay, are you ready?" Jen responded emphatically, "Yup, let's do it!"

And, all of a sudden, they ran out into the middle of our street and started dancing in the rain, shouting out exuberant expressions. Without a moment's hesitation, I joined them in dance with heartfelt abandon. And I joined in full heart with my unconditional and strong loving, Grace, and my beloved birth self, Clarity. We celebrated joyfully as the clear, crystalline, full spectrum waters poured down in buckets of blissful surrender. I was soaked in love.

The purifying waters of the ions had washed away my clouded impurities. My "oils" were cleansed, and soon the sun was shining brightly. Ripples of rainwater glistened in the light. I relaxed with Sister Grace, in *clarity*. I'm sure glad I didn't make other plans that beautiful summer day I drove to the beach.

Chapter Thirty-Two

Becoming 'Guru'

As I've moved along in my journey of remembering, I would like to share some personal examples of connecting to my divine oneness. All of these examples have helped me move toward my return to grounding love in the heart and the rebirthing of Clarity. In the first example, I must begin by setting the stage from an earlier standpoint.

I stated earlier that there was a time in my life when I was frustrated with an accumulation of various spiritual teachers who didn't seem to be very conscious in their own spiritual work. Having challenges with my small self's attachments at that time, I wrote a poem reflecting my emotions in an effort to release my distressed feelings. I called it "Purple Guru":

I yearned for the purple guru, the purple-aura'd one,
'cause purple after all is the color of knowing
and white may be too much to hope for.

So, I choose the purple guru; the one any true yogi

would surely emulate. Yes, the purple guru;
my soul had bled from all the other colorful guru dung.

I played my own peek-a-boo game with them—
they never knew I saw them true,
naked in their clothes of many colors.

And of fairies and gnomes, ghosts and goblins—
who am I to deny their fair stay,
as they debate over whether I am real or not?

I ride around in this tombstone life,
shaking my head at all the dead people
so sadly trying to wake up.

I thought I had to fix my helpers and guides, if I was ever to resolve my own challenges. This was, of course, keeping with true Coyote Trickster form. Remember, Coyote is such a master trickster that he even tricks himself. So, in my self-trickery, I had been caught in the need to fix others rather than letting go and making my own well-being independent. I buffered with diplomacy, in order to fool myself further, "Will you please behave so I can do my work?!" I didn't realize the whole experience was already my "work." It was a lesson in self-definition and not ruling over others as a false god or making others mini-gods by basing my well-being on their behaviors.

I had been cheating myself out of my own divine resolution as long as I depended on their resolution. Later, I learned this is true of any relationship. My well-being comes from me and only me! I needed to become my own healing guru. Any distortion in that truth that I chose would only delay the peace and resolve I sought. For those who are unfamiliar, a *guru* is one who is considered to have divine wisdom and higher knowledge, and guides others in such pure spiritual truths. When we become our own guru, we awaken to the divine wisdom within ourselves and allow it to become our navigator. So, I continued to distill my soul work at the refinery.

A couple of years after I wrote the poem, I received a gift I was finally ready for. This gift was a happening, not a tangible object. It happened during a weekend retreat that I went to called "Flower of Life," a workshop developed by Drunvalo Melchizedek who teaches a meditation known as *merkabah* and considers principles of sacred geometry. *Merkabah* is a Hebrew word meaning "chariot" and is referred to as the "throne chariot of God."[27] Sacred geometry is an explanation of the divine universal order. We were practicing the *merkabah* meditation and I was in a meditative state. All of a sudden, a holographic image came into my third eye, our conduit for inner vision. The vision was me in a meditative posture like we were in at that moment. Simultaneously, a voice shot into my conscious awareness that said "You ARE the purple guru; it is you!" In that moment, my divine-connected higher self, in the "throne chariot," had spoken to me with the most loving and confirming of messages. I was filled with joy and felt connected to the divine perfection that we are.

I pass this on to you, my friends. You are your own guru. You are your own healing guide. You came here with the map and only need to know you've always had it. It's in your pocket; reach in and lead your life with divine, conscious intention aligned with who you are. You are the divinity you seek, and you are your own divine master. Each of you, here on this earth and in the soul that you choose, go to your refinery every day to re*fine* yourself, re-*find* yourself, and return to your heart in love. It is the most spiritually enlightening game of hide-and-go-seek you will ever play.

There is a Buddhist proverb reflecting this: "First there is a mountain, then there is no mountain, then there is." This is our sacred journey into self, through the lost self, and back to self again. Did you ever notice that "sacred" is only two letters reversed from "scared?" We are closer than we often think! Here is a poem I wrote, "Into the Soul," reflecting this sentiment.

Into the soul love rejoins itself
in an infinite celebration of oneness and perfection,

waves upon waves of affirmation and revelation.

Into the soul lie the whispers of truth,
unstained by the lost ego shape-shifters
who came in darkness groping and innocent.

Into the soul purity vibrates, and
refreshing soothing waters heal the severed heart
once pained from trying to know in amnesia.

Into the soul I rebirth my greatness
and bask in relief of the ultimate homecoming
as I release all that I never was.

And the pure light of divinity brings
truth, compassion, comfort, celebration,
and gentle knowing to all that I ever am.

The more we are able to connect with this loving, perfected source, the more we discover that it is the truth of who we are, and the more we understand that we are the light we have been looking for.

I will share two examples of the power of group energy to support our reconnecting to the divine source. When we are in group energy with everyone convening together to do conscious spiritual work, a synergy occurs.

Some of you may have experienced this. It is as if the energy in the room shifts in some way. It is the same experience of going into a place of worship and you notice that the energy feels different. You are feeling the higher vibrational energy of people coming together in prayer or to do other related forms of conscious spiritual work.

The first time I experienced this was many years ago in the course called "Awakening" that I mentioned earlier. We were in the middle of the retreat weekend, a culminating part of the course, and we had all been meditating for over two hours with techniques known as "Dynamic" and "Kundalini" meditation. Many of us, myself included, had been fasting for several days on juice and water only. Dynamic meditation utilizes intense deep yogic breathing that activates the body's energy flows, releases emotional stores, and promotes internal harmony. Kundalini meditation is a powerful energy meditation utilizing music, movement, and stillness.

We were dancing in the room blindfolded so that we would not judge ourselves and each other. All of a sudden, after meditating in the room for an hour with the music, in this meditative and fasting state, I experienced a holographic image shooting into my mind's eye. It was me dancing in the room like we were but my head was missing! Upon seeing this image, I became utterly elated; I felt a joy and a bliss that was indescribable to me. This was one of the first times I had truly let go. It connected me to the heart, and I was in love! There was no "not perfect." Everything was right and needed no reason. Reason just was.

So to get ahead, you have to lose your head! Now you don't necessarily have to fast and do the same meditations to feel your heart burst open in love, though such intense group experiences can cut right through your ego defenses and take you right to the "heart of the matter."

What followed, at the end of these quite intense and energetic meditations was even more enlightening to me. Jessica instructed us to lie down on the floor with our feet facing in toward each other like a human wheel with spokes. She further instructed us to connect physically, for instance by touching a hand on another person's leg. I cannot describe perfectly in words what happened as we lay there, all connected, but I will do my best to convey it. I felt a deep and encompassing sense of bliss and pure love, the kind of love that says everything is perfect, that there is no wrong thing. In that moment, I was completely in love with life, every human being in it, and myself, more wholly than I had ever experienced. The feeling strengthened and intensified to the point that my body actually began to physically vibrate. It became so strong, that it was as if I *became* the vibration. I felt as if I could even hear it. Its intensity became so pronounced that, for a moment, I lost my God-connected self and went into a flash of fear.

I know now that this was the moment when my small self became afraid of losing itself. At that point my body pulled out of this intense vibration of energy. When I tried to get back to this experiential state, I was unable.

Can you get the magnitude of the collective gift we all are to each other? We truly can lift each other up. We need each other! We are each other!

The second example I will share reflecting this synergistic power of group energy occurred in more recent years. I was meditating through Siddha Yoga chanting during a weekend retreat at an ashram, Shanti Mandir, in Walden, New York. The ashram was located on 3,000 beautiful serene acres. An *ashram*, for those of you unfamiliar, is a Hindu place of sacred prayer and worship. Every morning we were lulled awake by the most beautiful recorded chanting filling the air. We would go down to a stream where the ashram community had constructed an outdoor kitchen, and we shared a delicious Indian meal. After happily burping paneer (a delicious homemade cheese) and other tasty food, we would do *seva*, a practice of selfless service, and then begin our day of meditation.

The energy had been building by the second full day in the ashram. I don't understand Sanskrit, the ancient Indian language we were chanting, but it has been explained to me that the vibration of the words, even without knowing the direct meaning, supports the individual in connecting with the divine source.

I received a direct experience of this during the second day. In the middle of chanting, I felt myself begin to lose my sense of physical form. As I chanted, I looked into the eyes of the other chanters and experienced an overwhelming feeling of love—I was every person in that room and they were me. I felt myself melting into them, and they were melting into me. It was as if our physical forms were becoming formless and fluid. This was one of the most profound feelings of oneness that I have ever experienced. I was so deeply in love, there was no "not love."

There are many conscious group practices that can lead you

to this point of spiritual awakening. Make sure that you are discerning in your heart. The approach must feel right for you, and the leaders must feel to you that they are grounded in integrity.

In addition to group practices, there are many supportive practices that you can do without a group that can also support you in your conscious spiritual work. What follows are several examples from my personal journey to awakening.

The first one can bring precious gifts when it arrives. I am speaking of being in a dream state where it's as if you have entered this state consciously while the dream is unfolding. This is known as "lucid" dreaming and there are methods to make this happen with conscious intention. You may look into this further to learn about how to intentionally guide yourself into lucid dreaming.

I recall two dream experiences where I became lucid. The value of lucid dreaming, and of pursuing this as a tool for your conscious awakening, will become clear from the examples below.

In the first dream, Jesus appeared before me. I realize my declaring this may seem a bit extreme. I am not attached to whether this appearance of Jesus was literal or symbolic. I can only tell you that it felt completely real. In the dream, I experienced him as being in a state of motion, and I had the feeling that he had others on his agenda. Imagine that!

He spoke to me very clearly, "How can I help you, my child?" I got the immediate sense that I would only have a second to respond before he went on, so I quickly belted out, "I'm in my head too much." In an instant, he reached down and touched me as I felt him hovering above me. In that second, I felt my body lift off of the ground up toward him, weightless. I was afraid, and then I woke up. Oh, you can be sure I wanted to get back there but the instant was the gift given. Having been raised Jewish and not exposed to the Christian faith directly, this dream was utterly astonishing to me.

What I got from the dream was that Jesus gave me an experience of "not my head" and that it was up to me to stay with him in that energy as long as I was able, whether for a second or more. If Grace provides me such a divine and sacred opportunity like that again, perhaps I will be ready to go deeper and further. Divine love gives us what we are ready for on both sides of the equation from pain to exultation.

In the second dream, I got a message that was in the form of an instruction, a tool I could take with me into my life. I heard a voice directing me to a pyramid and got a flash of the one on the back of a dollar bill, as if to help me visually connect with what was about to be conveyed. The voice instructed me to meditate inside the capstone in the top of the pyramid, and revealed that in there, I would receive an answer to any question that I put forth.

Prior to that dream I was unaware of a capstone on the pyramid. So, upon awakening and remembering this dream, I immediately pulled out a dollar bill and was amazed to discover that not only is there a capstone on the top of the pyramid but that it is levitating right off the top of the pyramid with energy lines under it!

I've since wondered if the capstone is a portal that transports us to either other dimensions or to our extraterrestrial cousins. I will need to spend more time meditating in this capstone. It is only in the joy of writing this book that my memory was triggered back to this dream, though I had described it in my journal the year that it came.

Again, the divine source had given me a precious gift, but it was up to me to be ready to use it. Perhaps in my next book to you, my beloved readers, I will have more to share about this capstone meditation experience. I hope, however, that you will not wait and will try this meditation on your own as a tool to be shared from our divine source. It is up to you as well to be ready to use it for what sacred gifts it may bring.

Hiring a practitioner who offers energy modalities is another way to support your soul journey on an individual level. Energy modalities offer support in balancing our energy centers in order to heal, ground, and solidify our well-being. This may include Reiki, sound healing, Sol-Core meditation, holographic re-patterning, chakra-balancing modalities, or Rho-Hun to name a few. With the Internet, it is very easy to learn of these opportunities. Again, I remind you, dear readers, to always be discerning in the heart when you choose. Make sure the description of the practice resonates with you by checking in on a heart level. That way, you can sense whether or not the energy of the practitioner is grounded in integrity.

You can muscle-test, as described earlier, or you can also test this by use of a pendulum. Just as with muscle testing, your inner, guided, divine self always knows what is for your highest good. Both methods serve as a connecting force to the energy of our higher knowing. If you are new with pendulums, Hanna Kroeger, in her book, *The Pendulum Book* (Hanna Kroeger Publications, 1973), gives a good overview of their use.

One of the methods I chose to support my conscious awakening was sound healing sessions. I hired a woman who I experienced as highly intuitive. Barbara used tuning forks and toning with her voice to help balance the chakras. Remember from earlier, our chakras can be on over-drive, "under-drive," or balanced.

During a number of sessions with her, while lying on the massage table, I would receive holographic images in my third eye that became precious gifts to me in my awakening journey. At one point, I received a vision of a beautiful golden chalice. The chalice was cupped by two hands radiating a most vibrant and bright white light; the hands gave the chalice to me. I was filled with a feeling of perfected love and rightness, a feeling I was becoming more and more familiar with. My heart wanted to burst open with the magnitude of this all-encompassing love.

In another session, I received a similarly sacred gift, the appearance of a golden orb that looked like the Egyptian orb often depicted above the heads of pharaohs and queens. Again, I experienced a perfected feeling of all-encompassing love and rightness. In yet another session, I saw an image of me lying down with a vibrant and lush green garden sprouting out of me along my chakras; I received the phrase, "I am a garden of light." Peace filled my spirit along with a sense of being fully present.

Another compelling image came to me during one of the sessions that soon led me into a meaningful adventure in sacred geometry. This time I saw an image of myself surrounded by what looked like two triangles inverted into each other. My arms were entwined like a double helix reaching upward, and there were beams of heavenly light extending out from around my head, arms, and the triangles. I felt the same feeling that I had experienced in other heightened awakening experiences. I came into a state of utter love and an overwhelming sense of divine perfection.

I told Barbara about it, and she said to me, "Caren, you have no idea what you have just experienced." She told me I needed to paint it. My small self protested a little, but I knew I had experienced something very significant; I had to explore it further. In the following week, I painted it as I saw it.

While I was in the process of painting, which was an utterly joyful experience, something else began to happen. While relaxing before bed at night, I kept getting a flash of the cover of *The Ancient Secret of the Flower of Life*, (Light Technology Publishing, 1999) by Drunvalo Melchizedek. The book had been in my possession for about ten years, but I had never actually read it, short of thumbing through it a bit at times. I had regarded it as a book to eventually hunker down and read, but I hadn't yet done so. Sometimes, we are planting seeds in our lives for future times when we are ready to reap the fruit of those teachings. After a few repeated times of this book's cover appearing in my mind's eye, I knew I had to pay attention.

One night, I fished it out of my beloved collection of books for the soul. I turned to the second page of the first chapter; my mouth dropped open and I gasped. There in front of me was almost the exact image I had sketched and had now painted. It was the Leonardo da Vinci image known as the "Vitruvian Man," with additional inverted triangles and directional lines rendered into it!

I leaped out of my bed and bolted over to my computer. I was excited because I was aware that Drunvalo Melchizedek had created "Flower of Life" workshops that went along with his teachings in the book. I had known that he had trained practitioners that led "Flower of Life" workshops and I felt the power of this synchronicity leading me right to it. I searched the Internet and was immediately led to the "Flower of Life" website and a listing of their workshops.

Yes! They still held workshops, and I discovered that one was being held in Northern Virginia, only an hour from my house, in exactly two weeks from that moment. This would be during my forty-fifth birthday weekend! It was a no-brainer. I immediately signed up. The meditation and lessons of sacred geometry that I learned from participating in the "Flower of Life" workshop has become another sacred and valuable tool in my journey of awakening. During a second "Flower of Life" workshop, just last summer, I awoke to my inner "purple" guru.

And so, my dear readers, divine love gives us our seeds to sow even when we don't know we are planting them for those moments when we are ready to reap them. You can now appreciate the true divinity of the Bible verse from Galatians VI: "Whatsoever a man soweth, that shall he also reap (*KJV*)." Remember "flower power," and infuse your "flower" with the sacred water of your true self. We are all "flowering" into the unfolding of our divine, loving essence, and we sow and reap our seeds along the way. Clarity guides us to return.

A year ago last spring, in the amazing red rocks of Sedona, Arizona, I experienced another sacred gift as I awakened further to my inner guru and opened to the divine source. I had fallen in love with the area and its amazing energy during a previous stay. Little did I know that my mother, who had selected Sedona for our mother-daughter spa vacation, would introduce me to a place that would hold deep meaning for me. Sedona would further support me in my journey of awakening in ways unknown to me at the time. Perhaps in our deep connection that we have shared as mother and daughter, she intuitively connected to a place that I was meant to know.

I returned last spring for a second trip to become further acquainted with the vortex energy of the red rocks. I planned for a week of hiking there in hopes of being able to slow down my monkey brain, arrive in one space to breathe, and *still* myself more fully to connect deeper with my essence. One of the things that inspired me so much to return to the area had to do with the previous trip with my mother.

Mom is a very open soul. She used the occasion beautifully, unfolding in her own quiet, peaceful, loving, and receptive manner, finding her way in her own self-loving fashion.

Mom and I decided to hike to Bell Rock, one of the known vortex sites. We hiked a mile to the rock, and Mom stayed at the bottom of the rock to relax and just be with the beautiful day. I myself decided to hike up toward the top where I had heard the vortex energy is stronger. I wanted to have a conscious experience of the energy, but my small self unconsciously feared the very enlightenment I sought. Adding to this unconscious distraction from my small self, I did not want to leave Mom very long. I told her I'd be no more than an hour.

So, I became "Ms. Monkey Brain" as I climbed and stayed up in my head. You might recall earlier, I named our ruminating, distracted, mind-chattering voice, the "monkey brain." When I got about two-thirds of the way up, "monkey me" only had about five minutes for enlightenment before I had to come down. It may have been helpful had I recalled, at that moment, the lyrics of a song by Simon and Garfunkel, "Feelin' Groovy":

> Slow down, you move too fast. You got to make the
> morning last...
> Hello lamp post, whatcha knowin'? I've come to watch
> your flowers growin'...
> ... feelin' groovy...

Wow, enlightenment in a lamp post?! In my monkey state, I did not have enough time to practice the fine art of "Zen lamp-posting!" I paused for a self-determined five minutes to sit down. Okay, okay, breeaathe, *ohmmmm*, breeaathe, *ohmmmmm*, fingers out and the middle one forming a loop with my thumb, can't hurt, okay contain the energy loop, breeaathe, *ohmmmmm*, okay gotta go.

Have you ever rushed enlightenment? Hmm, did I feel anything? Ummm, *ohmmm*, nahhhh! So, you may lovingly smile, and then perhaps connect with your own "monkey." Aren't we all so cute?

I hiked down to the bottom of Bell Rock where Mom just seemed to be basking in the light with a huge loving smile covering her face, a smile that has always been her hallmark. I received much more in joyful and loving feelings from her radiant smile than my five minutes of "*ohm*."

It wasn't until later during the plane flight home that she said to me, almost bashfully, "You know, Caren, I think I may have felt that vortex energy that you spoke of." She pronounced the word as if it was unfamiliar to her. "Tell me what you felt, Mom," I curiously responded. She appeared reflective and said, "It was like gentle, swishy wind." She smiled as we flew home.

Mom helped me realize how very much more I needed to slow down. When I set off for Sedona a second time, I was sitting on the red rocks of Oak Creek in Crescent Moon Park, looking ahead to Cathedral Rock. I relished her astounding reflection in the waters of Oak Creek. Before the first trip to Sedona, I had felt a calling to Cathedral Rock. When I first picked up books on the red rocks of Sedona and their vortex energy, I remember a tingling vibration that coursed up and down my arm when I read about her. Her energy felt very feminine to me.

On this day, gazing at Cathedral Rock gazing at me, I was in a peaceful, calm, present, and receptive state. I closed my eyes, taking in the energy of her splendor and the splendor of the overall area. It was then that I heard a very strong feminine voice. I sensed deeply that Cathedral Rock was talking to me. Her tone felt very commanding, but loving. My analytical left brain wanted to protest in unfamiliarity, but the connection I felt to that beautiful voice was too deep to deny. So I listened.

"Caren, put your hands in mine," she spoke lovingly to me. As she spoke, I saw immediately through my mind's eye two large, orange-red, mitten-like hands extend out of her orange-red rock body. For an instant, I hesitated and asked, "Which way do I put my hands?" She was quiet and I felt her simply smile a loving smile. I put my hands on top of hers and in that instant, I felt the whole essence of my energy swirl quickly up into her majestic and powerful, divine, earth body and shoot up out of the top of her crown. I felt and saw beams of bright vibrant light emanating out of her and I was deeply exalted.

My sense of physical body disappeared and a sense of heaven on earth beheld me. I stayed with this in reverence and awe for several moments, breathing and being fully present to her divine gift.

I know now that when we are present to such divine gifts, *we* become a "present" to *them*, as we return the gift of ourselves to divinity. The divine pure loving connection to be had within such an experience is immeasurable. It is why we are here! We are here to truly return:

Hashivenu Adonai elecha vena-shuvah, kadesh, kadesh yamenu, kadesh yamenu kekedem.

Help us to return to you, oh Lord, for then shall we truly return. Renew our days as in the past.

I opened my eyes. I was at one with my divine, beloved, earthly mother. Slowly and peacefully, I started to get up. As I stood and turned to leave, she beckoned me and said with the deepest and strongest love of Clarity and Grace, "Not yet, Caren...not yet." I turned back toward her and sat down in her lap. She smiled in heartfelt, God-connected love, and we exchanged our gifts.

Denouement

Ripples shimmy and glide the brilliant water,
going somewhere, where?
They glow.

Celebrating life, basking under the gold-dipped sun,
they wriggle, restless.
Where do they go?

Wading time to catch a destined path,
but there's a secret
and they know.

To find their way within themselves,
to reach inside
the soul...

and they let go.

    —Caren, age 18

Glossary

Addiction: The inability to be at peace with oneself, which causes one to fill from the outside with external satisfactions that are superficial and ephemeral. This creates a repetitive pattern in which the true self becomes repressed as the false self reaches externally to fill internally.

Ashram: A Hindu place of sacred prayer and worship where gatherers chant in the ancient Hindu language of Sanskrit.

Becoming your own guru: Becoming the master of your own healing and trusting yourself as your own healing guide.

Chakra: Sanskrit word for "wheel" or "turning." Centers of vibrational force that exist within the body, and that have an effect on our emotional, spiritual, mental, and physical states. They are known as the body's "vortex centers."

Clarity: Our original birth name, as we arrive here on earth in a state of divine connection and knowing.

Codependence: A state of being in which one's well-being is dependent upon the behavior and actions of another.

Coyote Trickster: Ego-based, fear-based, small false self. Coyote is the master ego shape-shifter who wants us to believe he is the true self. In Native American traditions, he is the master trickster coming to teach our life lessons as he even fools himself.

Divine frequencies: Also known as Solfeggio tones; original sound frequencies used in ancient Gregorian chants, said to create spiritual blessings.

Divine nature: Our God-given state of being in which we are all one. Our true nature in which there is no separation and we exist as a microcosm of God. Our true essence. A bottomless cup that never ceases to fill from the oneness of which it is essentially a part.

Divine oneness: Our true God-connected relationship to each other. It is the opposite of the illusion of separation. The state of living in our divine nature. God.

Divine self: Our God-connected self. The state in which we are born. Our true self.

Divine source: God.

Duality: A false state of separation in which we experience opposites. A fall from oneness. It represents the illusion we are here to resolve.

Dynamic meditation: A meditation utilizing intense deep yogic breathing that activates the body's energy flows, releases emotional stores and promotes internal harmony.

Ego: This is what forms the false self or small self. It is earth-based only, and does not come from our divine source. We create it to protect ourselves from our insecurities.

Elf: Mischievous little creature, synonymous with small, false, fear-based self.

ELF: Extremely Low Frequency of around 60Hz.

Emotion: Energy in motion.

Energy work: An alternative healing modality for emotional well-being, often utilizing sound or touch.

False self: See small self.

Fractal: Patterns of self-similarity that infinitely repeat from the micro levels of our existence to the macro. Their never-ending patterns can be measured with mathematics.

God: Love, oneness, divine source, infinity.

God-effect: The collective effect of love-based ripples and total absence of fear-based ripples. The resulting effect of everyone on the earth living in a state of oneness, where the illusion of separation is resolved.

Grace: Also known as "Sister Grace." She brings our more difficult soul lessons, unsparingly, to resolve ourselves fully into love. She brings temperance in the form of "saving graces."

Grand circle: The completion of our journey from birth in a state of true divine knowing and love, into a state of amnesia and forgotten divine self where we are lost in the fear of the small false self, and back to a state of divine knowing and love.

Grand illusion: The illusion that the false self or small self is the true self.

Grand journey: The journey home to the heart and unconditional love where we are reconnected to our divine nature.

Guru: One who is considered to have divine wisdom and higher knowledge, and guides others in such pure spiritual truths.

Higher self: Your inner guide.

Humanoid: A self-sabotaging aspect of self, addicted to negative thought patterns and the false projected belief that inner happiness is dependent upon the responses of others.

Hundredth monkey: The one that tips the scale of mass consciousness into a collective state of change.

Hundredth Monkey Phenomenon: When the "hundredth monkey" is reached, mass-consciousness is affected, and mass change occurs.

Illusion of separation: A state of confusion, born of the ego-formed false self, in a forgotten state of our divine nature. It is the opposite of divine oneness.

In lakech: Mayan phrase that means "I am another yourself; you are another myself."

Infinity: Complete unconditional love, which can never really be complete because it wants more and more of itself. The nature of our universe and of God.

Kundalini meditation: a powerful energy meditation utilizing music, movement, and stillness.

Love: Pure unconditionality; God.

Lucid dreaming: The experience of entering into your own dream-like state consciously as if you are in the dream as it is unfolding.

Maharishi Effect: An effect which has repeatedly shown that it takes only one percent of the population to perpetuate mass change. This demonstrates that individual consciousness affects collective consciousness.

Merkabah: The Hebrew word for "chariot" or "throne of God." In Egyptian, it means "light spirit body." It is known as a light vehicle to carry the human spirit and body from ascension into higher dimensional levels of existence.

Monkey brain: Our ruminating, distracted, mind-chattering internal voice, prone to the fears and the negativity of the small self.

Original addiction: The addiction to our small fear-based self, whose urges come from the ego, that fears its own annihilation, and works very hard to protect itself.

Resonance repatterning: A method for resolving emotional energy constrictions and unconscious patterns.

Reverse ripple: The ripples we send inward, our emotional attitudes toward ourselves, which fuel what we then manifest in our lives.

Ripple effect: The author's use of this term refers to the ever-expanding effect of our thoughts and related emotions on the greater whole,

from self, to others, to groups, to countries, between countries, etc...
It is based on the fact that the emotional energies of the world repeat
from the micro-level to the macro-level.

Sanskrit: The ancient spiritual language of India in which Hindu
scriptures are written and chanted. The vibrational tones of the words
are said to affect one's consciousness.

Secondary addiction: Any addiction other than "original addiction."
This would be, for instance, addiction to drugs, alcohol, gambling,
porn, and sex.

Self-similarity: A repetition of similar patterns on all levels of existence from the micro-level to the macro-level, from the smallest par-
ticle to multiple universes, and from inner self to greater-whole.

Small self: A fear-based, confused aspect of self that is not a part of
our true divine nature. It is based in duality rather that oneness.

Solfeggio tones: See "divine frequencies."

Spilt-milk syndrome: The first moment, as children, when most of us
were taught some aspect of shame. This cultivates a belief that our
very selves are defective. It comes in many forms, but the concluding
line that is delivered is always the same: "You are bad, you bad boy
(or girl). You should not have done that." Whatever "that" is, doesn't
matter.

True self: Our divine God-connected self; essential self.

Ultimate accountability: To be accountable to our soul lessons and
commitment toward personal resolution.

Ultimate healing: To fully resolve the false fear-based self and return
that self to the heart for self-love and nurturing.

Ultimate living: To truly arrive home in the space of the heart, and
live grounded in the love of that heart-space.

Ultimate responsibility: To be accountable for the ripples we choose to send out. In this sense, we become guardians of ourselves, each other, and the earth.

Unibot: Those who are in a complete state of self-absorption.

Unisation: The opposite of a conversation, where the direction of the "dialogue" continuously refers back to oneself.

Uniship: A "ship" of one. The opposite of a relationship. The disempowered state of being lost in self-absorbed arrogance, relating only to oneself and therefore in a relationship of "one."

Bibliography

Barks, Colemam, translations by Coleman Barks with John Moyne, *The Essential Rumi*. New York: Harper Collins, 1995.

Barks, Coleman, translations by Coleman Barks. *Rumi, The Big Red Book: The Great Masterpiece Celebrating Mystical Love and Friendship*, New York: Harper Collins, 2001.

Bryant, Mark. *The Artful Cat*. Philadelphia: Running Press Book Publishers, 1991.

Dillbeck, M. C., Banus, C. B., Polanzi, C., & Landrith III, G. S., "Consciousness as a field: The Transcendental Meditation and TM-Sidhi program and changes in social indicators," *The Journal of Mind and Behavior* 8 (1987): 67–103.

ELF (extremely low frequency). Last modified August, 2009. http://searchnetworking.techtarget.com/definition/ELF.

"Gordian Knot," *Wikipedia, The Free Encyclopedia*. Accessed April 7, 2011. http://en.wikipedia.org/wiki/Gordian_Knot.

Gunter, Bernard, *Energy Ecstasy and your Seven Vital Chakras*. North Hollywood, CA: Newcastle Publishing Company, 1983.

Horowitz, Dr. Leonard. *Healing Codes for the Biological Apocalypse*, 2nd edition. Sandpoint, ID; Healthy World Distributing, 1999.

Institute of HeartMath. (n.d.). *Developing Your Intuition*. Accessed April 7, 2011. http://www.heartmath.org/free-services/solutions-for-stress/solutions-developing-your-intuition.html.

"Kahuna," *Wikipedia, The Free Encyclopedia*. Accessed April 7, 2011. http://en.wikipedia.org/wiki/Kahuna.

Masaru, Emoto and David Thayne (translator). *The Hidden Messages in Water*, illustrated edition. Hillsboro, OR: Beyond Words Pub Co, 2004.

Melchizedek, Drunvalo. *The Ancient Secret of the Flower of Life,* Volume 1. Flagstaff, AZ: Light Technology Publishing, 1999.

"Merkabah," *Wikipedia, The Free Encyclopedia.* Accessed April 7, 2011. http://en.wikipedia.org/wiki/Merkabah.

"Ripple Effect," *Wikipedia, The Free Encyclopedia.* Accessed April 7, 2011. http://en.wikipedia.org/wiki/Ripple_effect.

Samardzija, Djendi, "The Art of Fractal Energy." Accessed April 7, 2011). http://fraktalneenergije.com/energy.html.

Sams, Jamie, and David Carson, *Medicine Cards.* Santa Fe, NM; Bear & Company, 1988.

Vitale, Joe, and Ihaleakala Hew Len, Ph.D. *Zero Limits, The Secret Hawaiian System for Wealth, Health, Peace, & More.* Hobokon, NJ; John Wiley & Sons, Inc., 2007.

Watson, Lyall. *Lifetide.* New York: Bantam Books, 1980.

Williamson, Marianne. *A Return to Love, Reflections on the Principles of "A Course in Miracles."* New York: Harper Collins, 1992.

CHAPTER ONE

[1] "Kahuna," Wikipedia: The Free Encyclopedia, accessed April 7, 2011, http://en.wikipedia.org/wiki/Kahuna.

CHAPTER THREE

[2] "Ripple Effect," Wikipedia: The Free Encyclopedia, accessed April 7, 2011.

CHAPTER FOUR

[3] For more information on fractals, please consult Chapter 17, "You are Fractal in Nature."

CHAPTER FIVE

[4] "Developing your Intuition," accessed April 7, 2011, http://www.heartmath.org/free-services/solutions-for-stress/solutions-developing-your-intuition.html.

[5] Most of the information in this chapter is derived from the author's studied knowledge of chakras from over twenty years of participation in retreats and workshops. My presentation of this subject reflects mainstream interpretations, yet there are many interpretations on the subject. For further reading, the author suggests:

Barbara Brennen, *Hands of Light, A Guide to Healing through the Human Energy Field* (New York: Bantam Books, 1987).

Carolyn Myss, *Anatomy of the Spirit: Seven Stages of Power and Healing* (New York: Random House, 1996).

Donna Eden, *Energy Medicine: Balancing Your Body's Energies for Opti-*

mal Health, Joy, and Vitality (New York: Penguin Books, 2008).

[6] The information on the chakra locations, vibrational sounds, and physical attributes is summarized from:

Bernard Gunter, *Energy Ecstasy and your Seven Vital Chakras* (North Hollywood, CA: Newcastle Publishing Company, 1983).

The information on the chakra colors and their emotional attributes is gleaned from the author's studied knowledge.

CHAPTER SIX

[7] Leonard Horowitz, M.D., *Healing Codes for the Biological Apocalypse*, 2nd edition (Sandpoint, ID: Healthy World Distributing, 1999).

[8] Katherine Bless, "The High Heart and other In-Between Chakras," Vibration Magazine, *The Journal of Vibrational and Flower Essences* (Nov 2006).

[9] Reproduced by permission from Marianne Williamson, *A Return to Love, Reflections on the Principles of A Course in Miracles*, (New York: Harper Collins, 1992) 190-191.

[10] Translations by Coleman Barks, Rumi, *The Big Red Book: The Great Masterpiece Celebrating Mystical Love and Friendship* (New York: Harper Collins, 2001) 476.

CHAPTER EIGHT

[11] "Gordian Knot," accessed April 7, 2011," Wikipedia: The Free Encyclopedia, http://en.wikipedia.org/wiki/Gordian.

[12] "ELF," last modified August 2000. http://searchnetworking.techtarget.com/definition/ELF.

CHAPTER TWELVE

[13] Translations by Coleman Barks with John Moyne, *The Essential Rumi*, (New York: Harper Collins, 1995) 36.

CHAPTER THIRTEEN

[14] To understand muscle testing even further, the following website offers free information with the suggestion of a donation: www.naturalhealthtechniques.com/basicsofhealthmuscle_testing.htm.

CHAPTER SEVENTEEN

[15] Author's note: the information in this chapter on fractals has been derived from the author's accumulated and highly studied knowledge of fractals over the past twenty years. For further reading, the author suggests:

John Briggs, *Fractals: The Patterns of Chaos: Discovering a New Aesthetic of Art, Science, and Nature* (New York: Simon & Shuster, 1992).

Mario Livio, *The Golden Ratio, the Story of Phi, The World's Most Astonishing Number* (New York: Randon House, 2002).

Martin W. Ball, Ph.D., *An Entheological Guide to God, Evolution and the Fractal Energetic Nature of Reality* (Australia: Kyandara Publishing, 2009).

Mike Flynn, *Infinity in your Pocket, Over 3,000 Theorems, Facts, and Formulae* (New York: Barnes & Noble Books, 2006).

[16] Djendi Samardzija, "The Art of Fractal Energy," accessed April 7, 2011, http://fraktalneenergije.com/en/energy.html

CHAPTER EIGHTEEN

[17] Lyall Watson, *Lifetide* (New York: Bantam Books, 1980) 147–8.

[18] M. C. Dillbeck, C.B. Banus, C. Polanzi, & G.S. Landrith III, "Consciousness as a field: The Transcendental Meditation and TM-Sidhi program and changes in social indicators," *The Journal of Mind and Behavior* 8 (1987), 67–103.

CHAPTER NINETEEN

[19] Squidoo.com/doveofpeace , accessed April 7, 2011.

CHAPTER TWENTY-TWO

[20] The description of this dream research is to the best of the author's recollection; the source of the research is not known.

CHAPTER TWENTY-FOUR

[21] Joe Vitale and Ihaleakala Hew Len, Ph.D, *Zero Limits, The Secret Hawaiian System for Wealth, Health, Peace, & More* (Hobokon, NJ: John Wiley & Sons, Inc., 2007) 47

[22] Joe Vitale and Ihaleakala Hew Len, Ph.D, 48

[23] Joe Vitale and Ihaleakala Hew Len, Ph.D, 32

CHAPTER TWENTY-NINE

[24] Jamie Sams and David Carson, *Medicine Cards* (Santa Fe, NM: Bear & Company, 1988) 138.

[25] Jamie Sams and David Carson, 137.

CHAPTER THIRTY

[26] Jamie Sams and David Carson, 137.

CHAPTER THIRTY-TWO

[27] "Merkabah," Wikipedia: The Free Encyclopedia, accessed April 7, 2011, http://en.wikipedia.org/wiki/Merkabah

About the Author

Caren Appel birthed her writing career from twenty-two years as a personal empowerment and wellness therapist. She spent the most recent eleven years in private practice as a licensed clinical social worker. Her powerful yet heartfelt approach to wellness and personal transformation has come out of her work with her clients as well as soul lessons from her personal journey. Caren is a master in helping people become spiritual warriors as they embrace emotional honesty in a shameless and self-loving manner. It is from these experiences that she was compelled and inspired to write this book.

For the past twenty-six years, Caren has been an active participant of holistic and metaphysical practices including Reiki, sound healing, chakra energy work, various meditation techniques, and sacred geometry. These have added to the richness and depth she has brought to her clients and to her writing.

Recognized as an authority on drug abuse in the workplace, Caren has given presentations, has published several articles, and has served as a contributing writer and editor on the subject. She has also led storytelling workshops for personal transformation.

Caren has been writing poetry from the age of fourteen. Her poems were first published in *Young America Writes* when she was eighteen.

Caren was born and lives in the industrial town of Baltimore, Maryland, with her three cats. Having grown up in a historic steel town and being the daughter of a retired forty-three year master cabinet-maker, it is no surprise that she enjoys hobby work as a metal sculptor.